SCHOLASTIC

DAILY SPELLING TEASERS

AGES 7–11

EILEEN JONES

CREDITS

Author
Eileen Jones

Illustrations
Nick Diggory

Development Editor
Kate Pedlar

Series Designer
Anna Oliwa

Editor
Kathleen McCully

Designer
Mike Brain Graphic Design
Limited, Oxford

Project Editor
Fabia Lewis

Text © Eileen Jones
© 2008 Scholastic Ltd

Designed using Adobe InDesign

Published by Scholastic Ltd
Villiers House, Clarendon Avenue,
Leamington Spa, Warwickshire CV32 5PR

www.scholastic.co.uk

Printed by Bell and Bain Ltd

1 2 3 4 5 6 7 8 9   8 9 0 1 2 3 4 5 6 7

British Library Cataloguing-in-Publication Data
A catalogue record for this book is available from the
British Library.

ISBN 978-1407-10019-7

CONTENTS

INTRODUCTION

DAILY SPELLING TEASERS FOR AGES 7–11

WHAT IS *DAILY SPELLING TEASERS?*

Daily Spelling Teasers 7–11 is a collection of over 140 spelling activities for everyday use. The activities teach patterns that can help children to learn how to spell both high frequency and unfamiliar words.

The spelling teasers include word games, puzzles, riddles, rhymes, mnemonics and story extracts. The ideas are designed to be used flexibly, and many can be adapted easily to reflect children's particular interests or to make cross-curricular links. In addition, most of the activities can be differentiated easily to cater for differing levels of ability within a class group.

HOW IS IT ORGANISED?

It is widely accepted that children learn in different ways. Teachers need to use a range of teaching styles and materials to ensure that all children are given the opportunity to learn.

The spelling teasers have therefore been grouped into four chapters, each focusing on a different learning style, thus providing a multi-sensory approach to learning:

1. Visual (seeing)
2. Auditory (hearing)
3. Tactile (touching)
4. Kinaesthetic (moving)

WHAT DOES EACH SPELLING TEASER CONTAIN?

Each spelling teaser focuses on a different aspect of word level work such as spelling plurals, using prefixes and suffixes, and extending vocabulary through generating compound words and identifying word roots and derivations. The following information is also included within each activity:

Objective: This refers to the desired literacy skill to be developed.

Learning link: Where other learning styles feature in an activity, these are listed in this section.

Organisation: This gives information about the desired class arrangement for the activity such as a whole class, pair or group work. However, many of the activities can be adapted easily to suit different circumstances.

Resources: A list of any items or photocopiable resources needed to carry out the activity is provided. The list includes any items which are to be prepared in advance of the lesson where needed.

What to do: This section provides brief instructions for carrying out the task. Where possible, these have been directed at the children themselves.

Now try this: At the end of each spelling teaser, suggestions have been given for extending learning in that particular activity in future lessons.

Answers: Answers are given, where appropriate.

HOW SHOULD THEY BE USED?

The spelling teasers are designed to provide ideas for ten-minute activities which should help to develop children's spelling skills. Some activities are to be adult-led (by a teacher or teaching assistant). However, in many cases, the activities are ideal for self-directed learning by the children themselves.

WHEN SHOULD THEY BE USED?

The spelling teasers can be used at any time throughout the school day: to change the pace of a lesson; to reinforce specific spelling patterns; as a form of Brain Gym®; or to encourage children to think independently.

WICKED SPELL

OBJECTIVE: to spell common prefixes and recognise how they influence word meanings
LEARNING LINK: auditory
ORGANISATION: individuals or pairs
RESOURCES: a copy of 'The witch's spell' (see below); dictionary; paper and a pencil, for each child or pair

My, my, how you have pleased me! As a reward, this spell will make you very lucky.

When it is proper, you will appear. At grand meetings, you will be so polite. You will become amazingly tidy. Your shoes will fasten themselves, your belongings will place themselves, and your cape will zip itself. I will give you animals which you will trust: mature black cats that will obey every word you say, and an owl to lead you through the night sky.

In magic and flying lessons, you will be the perfect pupil! You will spell every word, and understand every instruction and so be able to fly. In races, your performance will always qualify you.

With my spell, it is possible to really succeed. I know you will like it.

WHAT TO DO

● Read the witch's good spell and notice the highlighted words.
● The witch, in a bad mood, now wants to make a bad spell.
● Do the wicked deed for her! On your own or with a partner, re-write the spell by changing the highlighted words for their word opposites. Do this the quick way, by choosing a prefix to add each time: 'un', 'dis', 'im', 'mis'.
● Use a dictionary to make sure you use each prefix five times.

NOW TRY THIS

1. List the words and their opposites under these prefix headings: 'un', 'dis', 'im', 'mis'.

2. Using a dictionary and reading book, add three to five more pairs of words to each list. Can you spot any similarities between the words that use a particular prefix?
3. Discuss your observations with your partner.

ANSWERS
displeased, unlucky, improper, disappear, impolite, untidy, unfasten, misplace, unzip, distrust, immature, disobey, mislead, imperfect, misspell, misunderstand, unable, disqualify, impossible, dislike

BUBBLE TROUBLE

OBJECTIVE: to identify words with the spelling pattern 'le'
LEARNING LINK: tactile
ORGANISATION: individuals or pairs
RESOURCES: photocopiable page 58; a pencil and a dictionary, for each child

WHAT TO DO

● Look at the page crammed with balloons. They seem to be getting out of control.
● End the trouble by popping them. To do this, solve the clue to each balloon's secret word, either on your own or with a partner.
● Write the answer in the balloon, and draw a hole to let the air out.
● Remember to use a dictionary to check your spelling.
● Write down the two letters you will keep away from these balloons in future, to avoid having too many words with the same pattern. Explain how you worked this out.

NOW TRY THIS

Use the same two mischievous letters to make your own *Bubble trouble* page of balloons for your partner to pop.

ANSWERS
1. kettle **2.** vegetable **3.** little **4.** simple
5. poodle **6.** icicle **7.** paddle **8.** circle
9. uncle **10.** puddle

WHAT'S HAPPENING?

OBJECTIVE: to recognise how the addition of 'ing' changes the spelling of verbs

LEARNING LINK: auditory

ORGANISATION: whole class; individual

RESOURCES: a large whiteboard with a list of simple common verbs written on one half and pictures of animals or people performing different actions drawn on the other; a small whiteboard and a marker pen, for each child

WHAT TO DO

● The teacher will draw a line to link two items on different sides of the whiteboard (for example, between 'dog' and 'skip').

● The teacher will ask: *What is the dog doing?* Supply your own answer in a sentence: *He is skipping.*

● The teacher will link other items together and ask a question about what is happening (sometimes it might be a very strange event!). Write the answer on your own whiteboard, always using the 'ing' form of the verb.

● Display your answers to the class. Does everyone agree?

● Make up and write your own unlikely happening sentences, using the 'ing' form of the verb.

NOW TRY THIS

In pairs, look at each other's sentences. Try to explain what has been happening to the spelling of the base verb. Share your conclusions with the class.

SNEAKY!

OBJECTIVE: to spell words containing silent letters

LEARNING LINK: auditory

ORGANISATION: individual

RESOURCES: a display of words as follows (each with the silent letter omitted): 'cha-k', '-nome', 'tom-', '-nat', '-retch', 'thum-', 'w-ine', 'plum-', 'fo-k', 'hi-h', 'w-ale', 'ha-f', '-rite', 'sa-mon', 'r-ino', 'crum-', 'ca-f', '-rapper', 'de-t', 'ans-er', 'w-en', '-nu', 's-ord', 'r-ubarb', '-naw', 'r-yme', 'cou-d', 'dou-t', '-narled', '-rong'; paper and a pencil, for each child

WHAT TO DO

● Look at the collection of 30 words with a single letter missing from each. Each missing letter is one of the following: 'w', 'g', 'h', 'b', 'l'.

● Write the words correctly, sneaking one of the letters into each gap.

● Now make a chart of five columns, with these headings: w, g, h, b, l.

● Write the whole words in the correct columns – six words in each column.

● Read the words aloud (perhaps to a partner).

● Now write an explanation for why the letters are called 'sneaky'. Can you suggest another name, beginning with 's', which describes the letters? (silent)

NOW TRY THIS

Add four new words to each column. Try to work out some rules about the sorts of words that some sneaky letters seem to prefer.

ANSWERS

w: wretch, write, wrapper, answer, wrong, sword

g: gnome, gnaw, gnat, gnu, gnarled, high

h: when, rhubarb, rhyme, rhino, whine, whale

b: tomb, thumb, doubt, debt, plumb, crumb

l: folk, could, half, salmon, chalk, calf

POLYGON PUZZLE 1

OBJECTIVE: to improve spelling by using visual skills

LEARNING LINK: –

ORGANISATION: individual

RESOURCES: photocopiable page 59 and a pencil, for each child

WHAT TO DO

● Look at the first polygon. Visualise moving some of the letters around to make a word, for example, 'peel'. Be careful to use only the letters in the polygon.

● As you picture a word, write it down.

● Try to picture some of the letters in a different order and write a new word.

● As you run out of ideas for one polygon, move on to the next.

NOW TRY THIS

Each polygon is also an anagram (all of its letters, used together, make a word). How many of the anagrams can you work out?

ANSWERS

1. asleep   2. reward
3. invent   4. wallet
5. because   6. sausage

NOTE FROM MR FORMAL

OBJECTIVE: to use the apostrophe to spell contracted forms of words

LEARNING LINK: auditory

ORGANISATION: individual

RESOURCES: a prepared note (see below) with numerous opportunities for written contractions; a pencil and some paper, for each child

I have no time to spare. I will see you in the café later. I am not sure when. In case I am very late, you had better take a book to read, or there is usually a free newspaper in the café. If you are in a rush, do not worry about me. Go on to the match on your own! I will walk to the café, but if I cannot see you, I will jump on a bus that will take me straight to the match. We are bound to find each other there. Let us hope so!

Fred Formal

WHAT TO DO

● Read the quick note sent by Mr Formal to his friend. Although he was in a hurry, he has failed to save letters by shortening words using apostrophes (contraction).

● In the note, highlight 14 places where Mr Formal could have used a contraction apostrophe.

● Write down each of these words in full in a list. Say them to yourself or a partner. Now try to say them more quickly and naturally: this is the contracted form.

● Write down the contracted words, using apostrophes.

NOW TRY THIS

Compare each full word with its contraction. Circle all the letter(s) replaced by the contraction apostrophe.

ANSWER

I've no time to spare. I'll see you in the café later. I'm not sure when. In case I'm very late, you'd better take a book to read, or there's usually a free newspaper in the café. If you're in a rush, don't worry about me. Go on to the match on your own! I'll walk to the café, but if I can't see you, I'll jump on a bus that'll take me straight to the match. We're bound to find each other there. Let's hope so!

Fred Formal

LIMITED COLLECTIONS

OBJECTIVE: to use prefixes to create new words from root words

LEARNING LINK: auditory, kinaesthetic

ORGANISATION: individual

RESOURCES: a prepared worksheet for each child displaying four large postboxes, each with a different collection label as follows: 'in', 're', 'dis', 'de', and around the page a selection of 20 root words written in rectangles as follows (with a gap at the front of each word for a prefix): '-call', '-mist', '-arm', '-ice', '-turn', '-frost', '-play', '-soluble', '-build', '-infect', '-credible', '-allow', '-compose', '-visible', '-order', '-correct', '-visit', '-connect', '-code', '-dependent'; a pencil and a dictionary, for each child

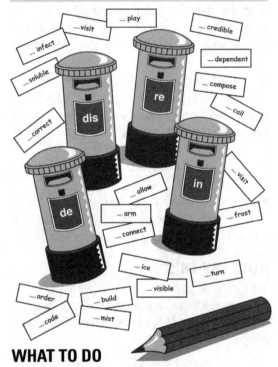

WHAT TO DO

● Each postbox only accepts postcards for words beginning with the prefix that matches its label.

● Complete the words by adding one of the prefixes each time. Use a dictionary.

● When you are sure your postcards are addressed properly, post five in each box by writing the full word in the correct postbox.

NOW TRY THIS

Act as postperson for someone else's mail. Exchange worksheets with a partner and check that everything is in the correct postbox. How much mail will not be delivered?

ANSWERS

in: incredible, insoluble, invisible, independent, incorrect

re: replay, rebuild, revisit, recall, return

dis: disarm, disinfect, disorder, disallow, disconnect

de: de-ice, defrost, decode, decompose, demist

HEADS AND TAILS

OBJECTIVE: to recognise and create compound words
LEARNING LINK: kinaesthetic
ORGANISATION: individual
RESOURCES: a collection of words which will form compound words arranged in two sets (see below) written on the whiteboard; a dictionary, some paper and a pencil, for each child

A Heads

hand   green
birth
play   ward
no
hand
care   clock
white
glow   life   some

B Tails

guard   worm
out
bag   taker
thing   stand
robe
house
one
room
day   wise

WHAT TO DO

● Read the collection of words.
● Work out which head will join which tail to make a new compound word.
● Use a dictionary to check that your compound word exists.
● Write each answer in the form of an addition word sum (for example: 'life' + 'guard' = 'lifeguard').
● Did you find any tails that were happy to join more than one head?

NOW TRY THIS

Look at three pages of your current reading book; the classroom notice board; your own writing. How many compound words can you find? List the compound words and then try to write them as addition word sums.

REPLY FROM MISS INFORMAL

OBJECTIVE: to use the apostrophe to spell contracted forms of words; to know that word contractions occur more frequently in informal language
LEARNING LINK: auditory
ORGANISATION: individual
RESOURCES: Mr Formal's note from 'Note from Mr Formal' (this activity can be used as a follow-up), paper and a pencil, for each child

WHAT TO DO

● Take the part of Miss Informal as you read Mr Formal's note. Are you satisfied with his arrangements? Decide what you will reply.
● Write your reply in rough.
● As your name suggests you are informal when you can be, so look for places where you can use contractions. (Reading the letter aloud, at speaking pace, will help you find them.) If necessary, change your note so that you have 10–14 examples.
● Write a final copy of the note.

NOW TRY THIS

Play 'Test a friend': exchange finished notes. Can you identify the letters that your partner has replaced with apostrophes?

POLYGON PUZZLE 2

OBJECTIVE: to improve spelling by using visual skills
LEARNING LINK: –
ORGANISATION: individual
RESOURCES: photocopiable page 59 and a pencil, for each child

WHAT TO DO

● Play a harder version of the polygon game.
● Check which letter is highlighted each time.
● Try to write at least two words from the polygon, making sure that you always use the highlighted letter.

NOW TRY THIS

Make up your own polygon, highlighting one letter. How many words can your partner make from it?

VISUAL LEARNING

ONE OR TWO

OBJECTIVE: to investigate rules for adding 's'
LEARNING LINK: auditory
ORGANISATION: individual; pairs
RESOURCES: list of singular nouns for each child, as follows: 'shoe', 'sandwich', 'berry', 'rose', 'delay', 'table', 'fly', 'box', 'ray', 'tune', 'baby', 'watch', 'boy', 'glass', 'window', 'brush', 'puppy', 'key', 'witch', 'day', 'tick', 'game', 'monkey', 'party', 'bush', 'army', 'toy', 'city'; a pencil and a dictionary, for each child

WHAT TO DO
● Read the list of singular words and think about how to make these objects' names plural.
● Write the plural form next to each one.
● Does the plural spelling look correct?
● Compare your results with your partner's. How do most words form a plural? Can you work out some helpful spelling rules?

NOW TRY THIS
1. Make five columns with these four headings: 's', 'es', 'ys', 'ies', and leave the last column heading blank.
2. Sort your answers into four groups, writing them (and their singular forms) in the column that matches their ending. For the final column, think of words that do not use 's' for their plural. What will you write for the column's heading?

> **ANSWERS**
> s: shoes, ticks, roses, windows, tables, tunes, games
> es: watches, glasses, bushes, boxes, brushes, witches, sandwiches
> ys: keys, days, rays, toys, boys, delays, monkeys
> ies: babies, parties, puppies, flies, berries, armies, cities

DETECTIVE WORK

OBJECTIVE: to recognise short words contained in longer words
LEARNING LINK: auditory
ORGANISATION: individual
RESOURCES: a list of words that contain other words within them (see below); colouring pencils and a dictionary, for each child

> **Word list**
> **1.** investigate   **6.** underneath
> **2.** shallowest   **7.** altogether
> **3.** greatest   **8.** clockwise
> **4.** prediction   **9.** operation
> **5.** different   **10.** quadrilateral

WHAT TO DO
● Prepare to act as detective and investigate what these words are concealing!
● Examine one word at a time, looking for shorter words within it. The letters of the shorter word must be in the correct consecutive order.
● Good detectives need proof! A dictionary will confirm if they are proper words.

NOW TRY THIS
Examine your results. Which long word produced the most other words? Did one short word keep recurring? Pool your results as a whole class. Discuss whether these hidden words will help you spell the longer words.

> **ANSWERS**
> **1.** invest, in, vest, tig, at, gate, ate
> **2.** shallow, shall, hallow, hall, all, allow, lowest, low, owe, we, west
> **3.** great, eat, at, ate, test
> **4.** predict, red, edict, diction, on
> **5.** differ, if, ere, rent
> **6.** under, eat, at, neat, neath
> **7.** alto, together, to, tog, get, ether, her
> **8.** clock, lock, wise, is
> **9.** opera, per, era, ration, ratio, at, rat, on
> **10.** quad, at, late, later, lateral, ate, era

MEMORY TIPS

OBJECTIVE: to investigate the effect of adding suffixes to words ending in 'f' and 'fe'
LEARNING LINK: auditory
ORGANISATION: individual; whole class
RESOURCES: the following words written on the whiteboard: 'curve', 'bluff', 'self'; a large sheet of plain paper and colouring pencils or felt-tipped pens, for each child; this activity can be used as a follow-up to 'Race the clock' and 'Scarfs and scarves'

WHAT TO DO
● Look at the words on the whiteboard. Say, write and check their plural forms.
● Use these examples and your own knowledge to list some general spelling rules for making the plurals of words ending in 'f', 'fe', or 've'.
● Share results as a class.
● Make a memory-aid spelling poster to help children with their 'fs' and 'ves' plurals.

NOW TRY THIS
English always seems to have words that break the rules. See if you can find and list unusual words (for example, beliefs, chiefs). Why are they unusual?

MAGIC DICTIONARIES

OBJECTIVE: to use a range of prefixes and understand their meanings
LEARNING LINK: auditory
ORGANISATION: pairs
RESOURCES: mixed-up list of prefixes and their meanings for each child, as follows: Prefixes: 'bi', 'pre', 'sub', 'ab', 'anti', 'non', 'mis'; Meanings: 'two', 'before', 'under', 'away from', 'against', 'not', 'wrong'; pencils and a stopwatch, for each pair

WHAT TO DO

● Write down two words beginning with each prefix.
● Discuss your list with a partner, talking about what your example words mean. Deal with one prefix at a time. Notice the repetition of certain words in your explanations. How does each prefix affect a word's meaning?
● Study the confused list of prefixes and their meanings, and work your magic by writing them in pairs. Use a stopwatch to see how quickly you can sort them.
● How instant was your magic?

NOW TRY THIS

Organise the prefixes and your word lists in alphabetical order.

PICK THE IMPOSTOR

OBJECTIVE: to explore homonyms
LEARNING LINK: auditory
ORGANISATION: individual
RESOURCES: a list of groups of three words (only two of the three being homonyms) for each child

---

Word groups (answers in brackets)
1. page, letter, biro (biro)
2. last, middle, lead (middle)
3. arms, crane, lorry (lorry)
4. yard, foot, mile (mile)
5. flat, new, book (new)
6. car, plane, train (car)
7. bracelet, ring, watch (bracelet)
8. wave, canal, bank (canal)
9. coffee, jam, spot (coffee)
10. bat, race, discus (discus)

WHAT TO DO

● Do you know what a homonym is? (A word that has the same spelling or sound as another, but a different meaning.)

● The words on the sheet are homonyms. Unfortunately, one member of each group has no right to be there.
● Put each member of the word group to a lie detector test! Make up two sentences, each containing the word that you are testing. In each sentence the word should have a different meaning. Find the word that fails to produce two sentences, and trap your impostor!
● List the impostors.

NOW TRY THIS

Can you replace the impostors with genuine homonyms? Let a partner try the lie detector test on your words.

RADIO WRITER

OBJECTIVE: to explore homonyms with the same spelling but multiple meanings
LEARNING LINK: auditory
ORGANISATION: individual
RESOURCES: story themes (such as: garden mishap; DIY disaster; school mystery; sea confusion); a list of homonyms (see below); paper and a pencil for each child

---

Homonyms
leaves, rose, gum, sound, row, bow, light, club, bank, pop, wound, grate, dear, table, spot, warm, safe, jam, plain, letter, stand, lead, ring, tug

---

WHAT TO DO

● Change your identity! You have been appointed as a writer for a children's radio programme called *Story for Today*. The producer has two requirements:
  1. The short story should be quite amusing, silly even.
  2. He needs to re-use your story in his school literacy slot so it must have about 8–10 homonyms.
● Remind yourself of what homonyms are (words that have the same spelling, but different meanings).
● List the homonyms that you will use, plan your story and get scriptwriting!

NOW TRY THIS

Tell a partner that you want to help the producer by highlighting the homonyms in your script. Can your partner identify them? Now put a special mark by homonyms that change sounds as well as meaning.

HIDDEN SECRETS

OBJECTIVE: to recognise short words contained in longer words as a spelling aid
LEARNING LINK: auditory
ORGANISATION: individual; pairs
RESOURCES: a teacher's (or teaching assistant's) name written on a large whiteboard (name must contain some hidden words of two letters or more); a small whiteboard, a marker pen, a pencil and some paper, for each child

WHAT TO DO

● Write this surname on your individual whiteboard: 'Jones'. Can you spot a short word of two letters or more inside it? ('on', 'one') Remember, the letters of the words must be in consecutive order.
● Look at the name on the class whiteboard. This name also has hidden secrets.
● Look at it carefully, searching for shorter words. Write down any that you find. Share your results with the class.
● Now consider your own name. Write it in full on your whiteboard. Can you find a hidden word of two letters or more in your surname or first name? Keep your results secret.
● Choose the best one of your names (the one with the most secrets). Write it on a piece of paper and exchange with a partner. Investigate each other's names.
● Report your answers to your partner. Did you find all their hidden secrets?

NOW TRY THIS

Share results as a class. Is the same 'secret' in many names? Which name gives the most words? Have any 'secrets' still not been noticed?

FOOL THAT EDITOR!

OBJECTIVE: to proofread work for spelling mistakes; to develop spelling strategies using contextual cues; to use a computer spell checker
LEARNING LINK: auditory
ORGANISATION: individual; pairs
RESOURCES: a list of newspaper headlines (such as 'Game of the century!'; 'School flood'; 'Grand final'; 'Mice mayhem!') written on the whiteboard; paper; a red pen and a pencil, for each child; computer access

WHAT TO DO

● Take the role of a newspaper journalist. Your editor is very fussy and is always putting red ink on your work. Get your own back by slipping deliberate mistakes into the newspaper.

● Think of some spelling mistakes that may be easily overlooked (for example, 'their' instead of 'there' or 'dominos' instead of 'dominoes'). Write a list of ten incorrect words you think the editor may fail to spot.
● Choose a newspaper headline and write a report of about 150–200 words, making sure you insert your ten deliberate spelling mistakes.
● Now pretend to be the editor. Exchange reports with your partner. How many mistakes will get the dreaded red pen?
● Explain to each other the checking strategies you used. How useful were visual skills? Were you alerted to a mistake by a word looking wrong?

NOW TRY THIS

Try the same trick on a computer spell checker: type your report and select the spelling tool. Does the computer find all the mistakes? Can you explain why it may have missed some? (The computer may not recognise that although the spelling of a word exists, it may not make sense in the context of your report.)

RIDDLE ME

OBJECTIVE: to examine the different spellings and meanings of common homophones
LEARNING LINK: auditory
ORGANISATION: pairs
RESOURCES: pairs of homophones written on the whiteboard (see below); a riddle added later (for example, 'I am an insect') written on the whiteboard; paper and a pencil, for each child

Pairs of homophones
be, bee; see, sea; heard, herd; place, plaice; right, write; hole, whole; great, grate; might, mite; new, knew; no, know; sun, son; weight, wait; deer, dear; threw, through

WHAT TO DO

● Look at the first pair of words on the whiteboard. Say them to your partner. What do you notice? (They are homophones, words with the same sound but different meanings or spellings.)
● Read the riddle and then choose the word that fits it. Does your partner agree?
● Look at the other pairs of words listed and write a riddle to fit one word in each pair.

NOW TRY THIS

Try to compose double riddles to apply to both of the homophones; for example: *It is my name, and helps me see* (I, eye).

ALL ABOARD!

OBJECTIVE: to recognise and spell the suffixes 'ship', 'hood', 'ness' and 'ment'
LEARNING LINK: auditory
ORGANISATION: individual; pairs; whole class
RESOURCES: a prepared worksheet for each child, with four columns, and a train carriage at the top of each column, labelled with a suffix: 'ship', 'hood', 'ness' or 'ment'; a pencil and a dictionary, for each child

WHAT TO DO
● You are going to help some words to travel by train! The train has four carriages, but each carriage can only transport words which match its label.
● Use your brainpower, a dictionary and a current reading book to find words that end in the suffixes that are shown in the carriages. Aim to write about eight words in each column.
● Think about the meanings of your words, discussing them with a partner. Talk about the root words. Has their meaning been changed by adding a suffix?
● Decide with your partner or as a class if the suffix has a general meaning.
● Share results as a class. Did anyone find a word with more than one suffix (for example, 'worthlessness')?

NOW TRY THIS
Look carefully at how the root words were affected by the addition of these suffixes. What spelling rules can you construct?

WORD SUMS

OBJECTIVE: to spell the endings of regular verbs
LEARNING LINK: auditory
ORGANISATION: individual; pairs
RESOURCES: a list of incomplete word sums written on the whiteboard (for example, 'shop + ed =?'); paper and a pencil, for each child

---

Word sums
shop + ed; try + ed; travel + ing; wash + s; hurry + ing; hurry + ed; hug + ing; save + s; spy + ed; stop + ing; show + ed; carry + s; drag+ ed; fry+ s

---

WHAT TO DO
● Complete the addition word sums on the board on your own.
● Watch out for any spelling pitfalls.

● Swap work with your partner to mark each other's sums. How many sums were right?

NOW TRY THIS
Discuss your results. What spelling changes were needed? Can you write down some spelling rules you have discovered?

ANSWERS
shopped, tried, travelling, washes, hurrying, hurried, hugging, saves, spied, stopping, showed, carries, dragged, fries

---

NOW AND THEN

OBJECTIVE: to spell words with common verb endings
LEARNING LINK: auditory
ORGANISATION: whole class; individual or pairs
RESOURCES: a verb list and sample poetry lines (see below) written on the whiteboard; paper and a pencil for each child

---

Verbs
carry, play, hug, drop, explore, rush, work, jump, drag, cry, look, save

Sample poetry lines
Now I carry a rucksack,
Then I carried a rattle.

Now I sleep in a bed,
Then I …

Now I play football,
Then I …

WHAT TO DO
● You are going to write a 'Now and then' poem. The poem will alternate between describing you now and describing you when you were small.
● Work as a whole class on an opening couplet.
● Now, individually or with a partner, write your poem in rough, dividing the poem into verses of 'Now' and 'Then' couplets.
● Read the poem aloud to yourself. Does the rhythm work well? Do some lines need more beats? Do you want to add any verses?
● Check the 'Then' verbs: do they sound right? Make sure you check any awkward-looking spellings.
● When you are satisfied, write out a neat copy of your poem.

NOW TRY THIS
Write a new 'Now and then' poem about your pet, family member or friend.

VISUAL LEARNING

WORDSEARCH

OBJECTIVE: to identify words ending in 'ough'
LEARNING LINK: auditory
ORGANISATION: individual
RESOURCES: a wordsearch prepared by the teacher with the following words hidden: 'bough', 'cough', 'rough', 'though', 'enough', 'although', 'dough', 'plough'; a list of hidden words (optional) and a pencil, for each child

WHAT TO DO

● You are going to do a wordsearch. The rules of this wordsearch are:
  1. Words may be written vertically, horizontally or diagonally;
  2. You may need to read words backwards;
  3. Letters must be in consecutive order.
● Search for words ending in 'ough'. There are more than five, but less than ten. The teacher may give you a list of words for which to search.
● Mark and list the words you find.

NOW TRY THIS

Select four new 'ough' words and hide them in a new wordsearch. Can your partner find them in four minutes?

SPOT THE DIFFERENCE

OBJECTIVE: to recognise common Greek/Latin roots in words
LEARNING LINK: auditory
ORGANISATION: small groups
RESOURCES: word sets (see below) written on the whiteboard; an etymological dictionary, paper and pencils, for each group

---

Word sets
decade, century, decimal, decibel
computer, telephone, television
spectrum, colour, spectacle, spectator
octagon, octopus, shark, octet
aquaplane, canal, aqualung, aquarium
spectators, audience, auditorium, auditory

WHAT TO DO

● In small groups, look at each set of words. One member of the set does not belong.
● List the words that are the odd ones out.
● Explain your selections to your group. Why do you think these words are the odd ones out? Decide as a group what the other words have in common. For example, do they all have the same root? Can you work out the meaning of each root? Use a dictionary to help you.

● Prepare a report to make to the class.

NOW TRY THIS

Listen as each group reports its findings. Did you always find the correct common root? Are you sure of its meaning?

ANSWERS
Odd ones out
century – from the Latin word *centuria*, meaning 'hundred'
computer – from the Latin word *putare*, meaning 'to hear'
colour – from the Latin word *colorare* and the French word *colorer*, meaning 'to colour'
shark – origin unknown
canal – from the Latin word *canalis* and the French word *chanel*, meaning 'duct'
spectators – from the Latin word *spectare*, meaning 'to look'
Roots
dec – 'decade' from the Greek word *deka*, meaning 'ten'; *deci* from the Latin word *decimus*, meaning 'tenth'
tele – from the Greek word *tele*, meaning 'far off'
spec – from the Latin word *spectare*, meaning 'to look'
oct – from the Greek word *okto*, meaning 'eight'
aqua – from the Latin word *aqua*, meaning 'water'
audi – from the Latin word *audire*, meaning 'to hear'

BACK AND FORTH

OBJECTIVE: to spell words with common endings
LEARNING LINK: –
ORGANISATION: individual
RESOURCES: a wordsearch prepared by the teacher, containing words ending in 'ial' and 'ight' (see below); a dictionary and a pencil, for each child

---

Hidden words
fright, flight, sight, slight, might, social, partial, trivial, cordial

---

WHAT TO DO

● Investigate the wordsearch to find and highlight the words listed. Remember they can go forwards or backwards.
● List five or six new words ending in 'ial' or 'ight'. Use a dictionary to check your spelling.
● Keep your words a secret!

NOW TRY THIS

Use squared paper to conceal some of your words in a wordsearch. Swap with someone else. Can you find each other's words?

WHERE'S YOUR HOME?

OBJECTIVE: to recognise common Greek/Latin roots in words
LEARNING LINK: auditory
ORGANISATION: pairs
RESOURCES: a list of Greek/Latin roots and their meanings (see below) for each child; an etymological dictionary and pencils, for each pair

---

Word roots
unus, geo, naus, ami, manus, vin, insula, specere, micros, voix, dictare, mal
Meanings
friend, small, to say, voice, bad, one, to look, hand, island, earth, wine, ship

---

WHAT TO DO

● Look at the Greek and Latin roots. These word roots have strayed into English but they want to visit their original homes. Help them by firstly looking carefully at the letters of the root and then saying it to your partner. Do you think the root looks and sounds as if it was originally French, Latin or Greek? Write down a country of origin for each root.
● Now match each root to its English meaning.
● Write down your ideas before using a special dictionary to find its true country of origin. How many were you right about? Did you find any from two languages?

NOW TRY THIS

1. Consider how the root is used in English. For each root, write down at least two English words that use it.
2. Be careful! The root will not always be at the beginning of the English word and it may lose or change some of its letters. Check! Are you still happy with your root and meaning pairings?

ANSWERS

Word root	Origin	Meaning
unus	Latin	one
geo	Greek	earth
naus	Greek	ship
ami	French	friend
manus	Latin	hand
vin	French	wine
insula	Latin	island
specere	Latin	to look
micros	Greek	small
voix	French	voice
dictare	Latin	to say
mal	French	bad

RACE FOR PAY

OBJECTIVE: to recognise and spell common suffixes
LEARNING LINK: auditory
ORGANISATION: individual
RESOURCES: a prepared worksheet for each child, showing five postboxes with a suffix on each: 'ible', 'able', 'ive', 'tion', and 'sion'; a dictionary and a pencil, for each child; a timer set for about 15 minutes

WHAT TO DO

● As a busy postperson, your target is to deliver six words to each postbox before your shift ends (when the alarm on the timer rings). You will earn points for each correctly spelled and placed word. (The ending of the word must match the suffix label.)
● Using dictionaries will take up time, but it will guarantee correct spelling. How much will you use your dictionary? You decide!
● When the timer starts, think of your words and write them in the appropriate postbox.
● When the alarm rings, stop and report your progress.

NOW TRY THIS

Become mail checkers as you exchange postboxes with one another and check the post. Are all words correctly spelled and placed?

TRACE OUR HERITAGE

OBJECTIVE: to recognise words ending in vowels other than 'e'
LEARNING LINK: auditory
ORGANISATION: individual; pairs
RESOURCES: a list of words from 'Strangely similar!' written on the whiteboard; an etymological dictionary, paper and pencils for each pair; this activity can be used as a follow-up to 'Strangely similar!'

WHAT TO DO

● Look at the list of words. Does their spelling seem strange? Why? Are they typical of English spelling?
● Discuss your views with a partner.
● Send the words back to where they came from! To do this, use an etymological dictionary to discover their countries of origin.
● Set out your findings in an interesting, eye-catching way.

NOW TRY THIS

Try to extend the lists with more words from your countries. Snowball into groups of four to compare results.

SPACE SAVERS

OBJECTIVE: to distinguish between 'its' (possessive) and 'it's' (contraction)
LEARNING LINK: auditory
ORGANISATION: individual
RESOURCES: a copy of the text (see below); paper and green and blue pens, for each child

Text

'It is too late now,' gasped Tanya. 'We'll never find the cover.'

They had finished playing with Tanya's new golf club and the cover of it was lying somewhere on the course.

'Everyone knows what the cover belonging to it looks like,' replied Darren. 'It is likely to turn up.'

'How?' said Tanya, despairingly. 'It is not connected to me by magic!'

Finally, they made a poster with a picture of the club and these words:

LOST: GOLF CLUB COVER.
It is brand new. The owner of it is Tanya Woods.
Phone: 00765432

'It is good to offer a reward,' suggested Tanya.

They added:

REWARD: a round of golf with the club belonging to it.

WHAT TO DO

● Remind yourself of the difference between 'its' and 'it's':
  ● 'its' means 'belonging to it';
  ● 'it's' is the contracted form of 'it is'.
● Read the text carefully.
● Then read it aloud, to yourself or a partner. Read the dialogue as if you are really speaking. Identify the five places where it would sound more natural to shorten 'it is' to 'it's'. Underline them in blue.
● Now search for five places where you could save space by using the possessive 'its'. Circle them in green.
● Re-write the text, remembering to obey your colour code and save space with the new words.

NOW TRY THIS

Discuss the results as a class. Try writing a sequel text with opportunities for your partner to practise their space saving.

ANSWERS

'**It's** too late now,' gasped Tanya. 'We'll never find the cover.'

They had finished playing with Tanya's new golf club and **its** cover was lying somewhere on the course. 'Everyone knows what **its** cover looks like,' replied Darren. '**It's** likely to turn up.'

'How?' said Tanya, despairingly. '**It's** not connected to me by magic!'

Finally, they made a poster with a picture of the club and these words:

LOST: THE COVER OF IT.
***It's** brand new. **Its** owner is Tanya Woods.*
Phone: 00765432

'**It's** good to offer a reward,' suggested Tanya. They added:

*REWARD: a round of golf at **its** club.*

SPELLING INVESTIGATORS

13.11.08

OBJECTIVE: to investigate, collect and classify spelling patterns in pluralisation
LEARNING LINK: auditory
ORGANISATION: individual; pairs
RESOURCES: class reading books; paper and a pencil, for each child

WHAT TO DO

● Use a few pages of your current reading book to hunt for plurals. List all the plurals that you can find.
● Aim to list about 20–30 words.
● Join up with a partner and combine lists.
● Can you find a clever way to group them? Keep in mind how their singular form has been changed/been added to.

NOW TRY THIS

Snowball into groups of four. Explain to another group how you sorted the words. Get together as a class to share conclusions.

SECRET AGENT J

OBJECTIVE: to form the plural of words ending in 'o'
LEARNING LINK: auditory, tactile
ORGANISATION: individual
RESOURCES: a list of plural spellings (see below) written on the whiteboard (see below); paper and a pencil, for each child

Plurals

heroes, banjos, dominoes, solos, zoos, volcanoes, flamingoes, discos, igloos, mangoes, videos, yoyos, echoes, pianos, casinos, haloes, buffaloes, patios, vetoes, torpedoes

WHAT TO DO

● Become a different person: Secret Agent Jake!
● Jake needs to be accurate: one misspelling could mean the wrong message.
● Jake uses his 'LSCWC' code to make sure he will always be correct.
● Try his code on the tricky list of 'os/oes' plural spellings shown on the board. Work on learning four at a time. Look at them; Say them; Cover them up; Write them; Check them.
● How long does it take you to learn all of the words and be ready for Secret Agent work?

NOW TRY THIS

Let a partner set you a spelling test (making sure that they ask you the words in a random order). Have you passed the Secret Agent test?

FROM LITTLE ROOTS 1

OBJECTIVE: to recognise word roots, derivations and spelling patterns
LEARNING LINK: auditory
ORGANISATION: individual; pairs; whole class
RESOURCES: a list of root words for oral work (see below); the following example sentence written on the whiteboard: 'Press with enough pressure to make an impression'; a small whiteboard and a marker pen, for each child

Root words

act, child, take, electric, hero, bore, pack, joy, cover, light

Sample sentences

● The audience reacted well to the acting in the first act.
● The child spent her childhood playing childish games.
● I take it that it was a mistake to overtake me!
● Electric plugs and electrical tools gave the electrician no problems.
● The hero performed an heroic act of true heroism.
● I will bore you if I tell you that boring story about my boredom on Sunday.
● Pack the papers in packets and place them in one particular package.
● The baby's joyful laugh of real joy gave enjoyment to his watching parents.
● Discover the hidden box, remove the cover and you will make the discovery of your life.
● Please enlighten me and tell me how lightning can affect my light switch.

Associated words in sample sentences

reacted, acting; childhood, childish; mistake, overtake; electrical, electrician; heroic, heroism; boring, boredom; packets, package; joyful, enjoyment; discover, discovery; enlighten, lightning

WHAT TO DO

● Read the example sentence on the whiteboard. Look carefully at it and write down what you notice.
● Compare your observation with a partner's. Work out your answers to these questions:
  1. Which three words are connected?
  2. What is their connection?
  3. Is the link in meaning, spelling or both?
  4. Which of the three words is the root word? ('press')
● Discuss answers as a class.
● Use your individual whiteboard to write down associated word(s) when your teacher calls out a new root word.
● Display and compare answers. Make sure they all have the double connection of spelling and meaning.

NOW TRY THIS

Use some of the associated words you have discovered to write sentences with three linked words, as in the original example. Highlight the root word each time.

VISUAL LEARNING

FROM LITTLE ROOTS 2

OBJECTIVE: to recognise word roots, derivations and spelling patterns
LEARNING LINK: auditory
ORGANISATION: individual; pairs
RESOURCES: children's own sentences from 'Now try this' in 'From little roots 1' or sentences provided by you (for example: 'In the first act, the actor had plenty of action scenes.'); a dictionary, for each child

WHAT TO DO

● Look at the sentences, each containing a root and two associated words.
● Focus on the three connected words in each sentence.
● Use a dictionary to help you work out their word types: are they nouns, verbs, adjectives or adverbs?
● Discuss your results with a partner. Do they always agree with you?

NOW TRY THIS

Create a chart with columns for the different word types. Enter your results, highlighting the roots. Do some root words have lots of gaps in the table? Can you think of associated words of different word types to fill in the gaps?

PRIZE COLLECTIONS

OBJECTIVE: to explore spelling patterns of consonants and formulate rules
LEARNING LINK: auditory
ORGANISATION: pairs; groups of four
RESOURCES: class reading books; paper and a pencil, for each child

WHAT TO DO

● Work with a partner, researching about four pages of two different reading books.
● Look for and write words containing these letter groups: 'ca', 'ce', 'ci', 'co' and 'cu'.
● Aim to list about six words per group. If you cannot find enough words, try another two books.
● Snowball into a group of four, and compare lists with another pair. Do you notice any patterns? Can you make any rules for words containing the letter 'c' followed by a vowel?

NOW TRY THIS

Work as a class to compile a display which shows your collection of words which contain 'c' followed by a vowel.

FATHER CHRISTMAS'S HELPER

OBJECTIVE: to learn to spell unstressed vowels
LEARNING LINK: tactile
ORGANISATION: pairs; whole class
RESOURCES: addressed 'parcels' (see below); parcels with incomplete addresses (see below) for the final part of the activity

---

Addresses for parcels
explanatory, reference, voluntary, stationery, factory, difference, embroidery, dictionary, jewellery, conference, category, secretary

Parcels with incomplete addresses
Infirm… ; preparat… ; dispens… ; abstin… ; imagin… ; condol… ; drudge… ; migrat… ; legend… ; rever… ; monast…

WHAT TO DO

● Look at Father Christmas's jumble of presents. To have a chance of delivering them on time, he must sort them into piles.
● Discuss sorting ideas with a partner. Agree on your best suggestion.
● Have a class discussion on how to sort the parcels (according to the endings of the words).
● Sort them into piles in the time allowed.

NOW TRY THIS

There are some more parcels which have incomplete addresses. Help Father Christmas by completing the addresses so they can each go in one of the piles.

ANSWERS
Sorted parcels
● ory: explanatory, factory, category
● ary: dictionary, secretary, voluntary
● ence: difference, conference, reference
● ery: jewellery, stationery, embroidery
Complete addresses
infirmary, preparatory, dispensary, abstinence, imaginary, condolence, drudgery, migratory, legendary, reverence, monastery

---

ARCHAEOLOGICAL DIG

OBJECTIVE: to investigate and learn spelling rules
LEARNING LINK: auditory
ORGANISATION: individual
RESOURCES: the word 'living' written on the whiteboard; a list of words to be investigated (see below); a small whiteboard, a marker pen, a pencil and a dictionary, for each child

Words for investigation
lovely, careless, hoped, shameful, rehearsal, surely, useful, tuneless, loving, pavement, useless

WHAT TO DO

● Look at the word 'living' written on the whiteboard. 'Dig' into the word and write down its base word on your whiteboard ('live').
● Hold up your answer. Does everyone agree?
● Do archaeological digs on the list of words and write down the base word of each. When necessary, check in a dictionary that you have made a real find and your base word exists.
● Did you unearth the same base word more than once? What do all the base words have in common?

NOW TRY THIS

List the suffixes that seem useful for creating new words from base words. Use the same base words, changing suffixes to create new words.

ANSWERS
Base words: love, care, hope, shame, rehearse, sure, use, tune, love, pave, use

THE ARCHAEOLOGISTS ARE BACK!

OBJECTIVE: to use suffixes to create new words from root words
LEARNING LINK: auditory
ORGANISATION: pairs; individual
RESOURCES: a list of suffixes (see below) and a pencil, for each child; this activity can be used as a follow-up to 'Archaeological dig'

Suffixes
able, ful, ed, ing, ment, al, less, ness, est, ism, ly, er

WHAT TO DO

● Talk to a partner about some of the suffixes added to base words in 'Archaeological dig' (if applicable).
● Now look at the list. How many had you thought of?
● Use the list to sort the suffixes into two types: vowel suffixes (ones that begin with a vowel) and consonant suffixes (ones that begin with a consonant).
● List six base words ending in 'e' (for example: live, hope, care, use, save, age).
● Experiment with adding different suffixes to the base words.

NOW TRY THIS

Look at the words you made by adding vowel and consonant suffixes to base words ending in 'e'. Write a spelling rule for each of the two types of suffix when adding them to base words ending in 'e'.

SAME START, DIFFERENT FINISH

OBJECTIVE: to recognise word roots, derivations and spelling patterns
LEARNING LINK: auditory
ORGANISATION: individual
RESOURCES: photocopiable page 60 and a pencil, for each child

WHAT TO DO

● You are going to write a poem with word-playing, tongue-twisting lines.
● Each line must contain three connected words that begin the same, but end differently.
● Use the opening line supplied, or make up your own.
● Make your editing easier by working in rough or on a computer.
● Polish and produce your final version.

NOW TRY THIS

Read your poem to a partner. Can they identify all your clever connections?
In groups, hold word-playing, tongue-twisting poetry festivals.

VISUAL LEARNING

NEGATIVE THINKING

OBJECTIVE: to recognise the spelling and meaning of words meaning 'not'
LEARNING LINK: auditory
ORGANISATION: individual or pairs
RESOURCES: photocopiable page 61 and a pencil, for each child

WHAT TO DO
● The clues to this crossword are very negative! Read them quickly. Can you see why? (They all contain the word 'not' or 'no'.)
● Study the clues and get busy finding the solutions.
● Write answers in rough first.

NOW TRY THIS
Imagine extending the negative thinking crossword. Write six extra clues. Try them out on someone else.

> **ANSWERS**
> **Across**
> **1.** Incorrect **3.** Impossible **5.** Illegal **6.** Improper
> **7.** Unlike
> **Down**
> **1.** Irresponsible **2.** Illegible **3.** Inactive **4.** Illiterate
> **5.** Irregular

MAZE RESCUE!

OBJECTIVE: to explore spelling patterns of consonants
LEARNING LINK: tactile
ORGANISATION: individual
RESOURCES: photocopiable page 62 and a pencil, for each child

WHAT TO DO
● There are 10 'ful' words lost inside the word maze ('pitiful', 'lawful', 'careful', 'hopeful', 'painful', 'useful', 'fruitful', 'armful', 'tuneful', 'mindful').
● Thread your way through as you hunt for them. You may take any direction you want (up, down or sideways), but you may never jump over a step.
● List the words that you rescue.

NOW TRY THIS
List at least ten other 'ful' words.

> **ANSWERS**
> mindful → painful → tuneful → useful → hopeful →
> armful → lawful → fruitful → careful → pitiful

GIVE AND TAKE

OBJECTIVE: to use and understand a range of prefixes
LEARNING LINK: auditory
ORGANISATION: individual; pairs
RESOURCES: the answer list from the 'Negative thinking' crossword for each pair; paper and a pencil, for each child

WHAT TO DO
● Look at the list of words. Underline the first two letters of 'irresponsible'.
● Discuss with a partner what the word means if you remove these two letters. What is the job of those two letters? (To create a negative form.) What is the name given to the two letters when used in this way? (A prefix.)
● Identify three other prefixes used in the word list.
● Create a chart of four columns, and give each a prefix heading ('il', 'in', 'ir', 'im').
● Enter the words in their appropriate column, like this: 'ir + responsible'.

NOW TRY THIS
Add about four new words with the appropriate negative prefixes to each column. Set the words out in the same way, making sure there is always a proper word left when you remove the prefix. Compare results with a partner.

DOING WELL!

OBJECTIVE: to identify mis-spelled words in own writing
LEARNING LINK: auditory
ORGANISATION: individual
RESOURCES: children's writing books; paper and a pencil, for each child

WHAT TO DO
● Think about your personal spelling mistakes. Investigate your recent stories, looking for repeated errors, and make a list of them.
● Set yourself a target to improve your spelling – perhaps 15 words to learn this week.
● Write two copies of that list, one to take home and one to display where you will see it in school (for example, you could make it into a bookmark).

NOW TRY THIS
1. Use your LSCWC code (Look, Say, Cover, Write, Check) to help you learn the spellings.
2. Ask a friend to test you.

DISCOVERY TIME

OBJECTIVE: to use word roots
LEARNING LINK: auditory
ORGANISATION: individual
RESOURCES: word sets (see below) written on the whiteboard; an etymological dictionary; a notepad and a pencil, for each child

Word sets

portable, porter, portfolio, portmanteau
microscope, microphone, microcosm, microbe
arachnophobia, claustrophobia, agoraphobia, hydrophobia
superlative, supernatural, superintendent, supermarket
autograph, telegraph, photograph, graphic
audience, audible, audition, auditorium
aeroplane, aerospace, aerodrome, aerofoil

WHAT TO DO

- Take on the role of word detectives.
- Look at the sets of words. Use your detective notepad to jot down your suspicions about them by answering these questions:
  1. How many families does a set of words seem to belong to?
  2. Do the family members share a common root? What is it?
  3. What do you suspect is its meaning?
  4. Does the root seem to be an English word?
- Confirm or reject your suspicions by using an etymological dictionary.
- Record the correct information about the meanings and, if possible, origins of the word roots.
- Assess your word detective skills.

NOW TRY THIS

Write, in a scattered, random order, a page of ten words, using the same roots. Show this new evidence to your detective partner. How quickly can they identify a word's root family? What do they know about its origin and meaning?

ANSWERS
Root words
Port, micro, phobia, super, graph, audi, aero
Meanings

port	carry
micro	small
phobia	fear
super	greater
graph	to write
audi	hear
aero	air

RACE THE CLOCK

OBJECTIVE: to use the endings 'f', 'ff' and 'fe'
LEARNING LINK: auditory
ORGANISATION: pairs
RESOURCES: a clock or stop watch; a dictionary; paper and pencils, for each pair

WHAT TO DO

- Check how much time your teacher has allowed (perhaps ten minutes).
- Make a chart with three headings: 'f', 'ff' and 'fe'.
- Work with a partner, brainstorming three lists of words that end in these letters.
- Write your lists, checking any spellings you are uncertain about in a dictionary.
- Which column is longest?

NOW TRY THIS

Divide your columns of words into nouns and verbs. Save your results for a future activity.

STRANGELY SIMILAR!

OBJECTIVE: to recognise words ending in vowels other than 'e'
LEARNING LINK: auditory
ORGANISATION: pairs
RESOURCES: a list of words (see below) written on the whiteboard; a dictionary, paper and pencils, for each pair

Words

ravioli, piccolo, emu, panda, armadillo, concerto, risotto, chapatti, banjo, tagliatelli, tarantula, viola, oratorio, spaghetti, gecko

WHAT TO DO

- Look at the list of words. Discuss their meanings with a partner, using a dictionary where needed.
- Group the words in topic categories (such as 'food', 'music', 'animals').
- Give each category an interesting heading.

NOW TRY THIS

1. Scrutinise the words, looking for something that they have in common. (Pay close attention to their final letters.)
2. You should have noticed that they all end in a vowel. Do some vowel endings occur more often in particular topics? Which vowel ending is never used? (e)

LIVE COMMENTARY

OBJECTIVE: to recognise how the addition of 'ing' changes the spelling of verbs
LEARNING LINK: kinaesthetic
ORGANISATION: individual; pairs; whole class
RESOURCES: sports commentary, containing frequent uses of 'ing' present tense verbs, to be read by the teacher (see below); paper and a pencil, for each child

Sample commentary

The game is *getting* fast. The centre-forward is *running* up the pitch. He's *slipping* the ball past every defender. Is he *going* to score? Only the goalkeeper is *standing* in his way. The fans are *clapping* and *cheering*. The goalie is *rubbing* his gloves together, *staring* at the ball. He must be *guessing* which way he should jump. The centre-forward is *taking* his shot. The ball's *coming*! The goalie is *leaping* the right way! Oh, disaster! The ball's *falling* from his hands! It's *rolling* over the line. United are *winning* one-nil.

WHAT TO DO

● You are going to listen to a sports commentary on a live sports fixture. Discuss with others how you think the commentator will make sure that you feel the event is really happening now.
● Ask a partner to say these two sentences to you:
  1. *The centre-forward runs fast.*
  2. *The centre-forward is running fast.*
● Which verb form sounds more immediate? (The 'ing' form is better.)
● 'Switch' on the radio and listen to today's live match commentary. (You will recognise your teacher's voice!) Count the number of 'ing' verbs you hear used. If possible, write them down. (If you work with a partner, one of you could count, while the other one writes down the verb.)
● Compare your results as a class.

NOW TRY THIS

Work with a partner, taking turns to give a short commentary on another live event (for example, a different sports event or a concert). Make sure you use plenty of 'ing' verbs so it sounds as if it is happening in front of your eyes.

ODD MAN OUT

OBJECTIVE: to identify words with the spelling pattern 'le'
LEARNING LINK: visual
ORGANISATION: pairs; whole class
RESOURCES: collections of words (see below) to be read out

Word collections

1. able, uncle, parcel, cycle
2. double, obstacle, small, mile
3. hole, simple, model, horrible
4. bicycle, nozzle, magical, table
5. tunnel, purple, sizzle, vegetable
6. real, possible, icicle, noodle
7. medal, responsible, wriggle, middle
8. poodle, sale, example, mural
9. little, medical, giggle, cubicle
10. towel, apple, miracle, trouble

WHAT TO DO

● Talk about words ending in 'le'. Remind each other of a few examples.
● You are going to listen to some collections of words being read out. For each collection, identify and list the words belonging to the 'le' family. In a separate list, write the odd one out.
● Work with a partner to investigate the words orally. What can you discover about the most common letters preceding 'le'? Which are common? Do you notice anything about the shape of many of them? (Most have an ascender or descender.)
● Compare results as a class.

NOW TRY THIS

List some words that end in 'cel' or 'cle'. Can you work out (by reading them aloud to each other) how you know which spelling is correct? (The 'c' is always soft in 'cel' endings, but hard in 'cle' endings).

STARTER FOR...

OBJECTIVE: to use different prefixes
LEARNING LINK: kinaesthetic
ORGANISATION: groups of three
RESOURCES: a list of prefixes: 'ex', 'in', 're', 'sub', 'non', to be read out

WHAT TO DO

● Form a group of three.
● When a prefix is called out, your group has to think of three words using that prefix. Discuss your answers with the rest of the group, but you must be ready to return your answers when the teacher points to your group!
● As the game progresses, your target number will increase gradually to four, five or six words.

NOW TRY THIS

1. Now form a group of ten. Play a game of 'Starter for ten': when a prefix is called out, your group must agree on a word for each of you to say when the teacher points to your group.
2. Discuss the meanings of the prefixes with the rest of the class.

MISTAKE!

OBJECTIVE: to become familiar with and spell some common prefixes
LEARNING LINK: visual
ORGANISATION: individual
RESOURCES: sets of words to be read out (one word in each set is incorrect; see below); a small whiteboard and a marker pen, for each child

Word sets
1. displease, disappear, distie
2. unhappy, unagree, unlucky
3. disconnect, disqualify, disice
4. decomposed, deofficial, decode
5. untidy, unmature, unseen
6. prebound, precaution, premature
7. rebuild, rewrite, reown
8. dishonest, dispick, disown

WHAT TO DO

● *I am feeling dishappy.* Can you work out what is wrong with this sentence?
● Now correct the sentence using the right prefix.
● The teacher will call out some other examples for you to correct (for example, beginning with the prefixes 're', 'pre', 'de').

● Now listen to some sets of words all using the same prefix (see box, left). In each set of words, one word has an incorrect prefix. On your whiteboard, write down the word that contains a mistake. Hold up your answer.
● Now write down the correct prefix for that word, and hold it up. Does everyone agree?

NOW TRY THIS

Continue the game in pairs. How many times can you catch each other out?

ANSWERS
1. untie **2.** disagree **3.** de-ice **4.** unofficial
5. premature **6.** rebound **7.** disown **8.** unpick

MARKING TIME

OBJECTIVE: to work out some basic rules for spelling changes when 's' is added to nouns
LEARNING LINK: kinaesthetic, visual
ORGANISATION: individual; whole class
RESOURCES: a list of singular nouns (see below); adult helper/teaching assistant

Singular nouns
fox, watch, key, sandwich, book, toy, glass, match, shoe, donkey, bench, day, church, wood, witch

WHAT TO DO

● The teacher says a familiar singular noun, and the teaching assistant says its plural. They demonstrate this routine several times.
● Now the teacher says another noun, and points at someone in the class, who should supply its plural.
● The pace will be fast, with the teacher pointing to different children.
● The singulars and plurals should be listed on the whiteboard.
● The list can also be used for a clapping game: the teacher claps and says the singular, the children clap and say the plural, indicating the correct number of syllables by the number of claps.

NOW TRY THIS

1. Repeat the clapping game with a partner. Consider: How many syllables in 'lunch'? (one) How many in 'lunches'? (two) Which sound makes the extra syllable? ('es').
2. Investigate other words. What can you discover to help you with your spelling?

AUDITORY LEARNING

MAKING RULES

OBJECTIVE: to work out some basic rules for spelling changes when 's' is added to nouns
LEARNING LINK: kinaesthetic, visual
ORGANISATION: pairs
RESOURCES: a list of singular and plural words (see below), paper and a pencil for each pair; this activity can be used as a follow-up to 'One or two'

Singular words

shoe, sandwich, berry, rose, delay, table, fly, box, ray, tune, baby, watch, boy, glass, window, brush, puppy, key, witch, day, tick, game, monkey, party, bush, army, toy, city

Plural words

s: shoes, ticks, roses, windows, tables, tunes, games
es: watches, glasses, bushes, boxes, brushes, witches, sandwiches
ys: keys, days, rays, toys, boys, delays, monkeys
ies: babies, parties, puppies, flies, berries, armies, cities

WHAT TO DO

● You will be given some groups of words to study. Talk to a partner about the similarities and differences in the plural endings. Say the words aloud to each other: hearing the differences will help you. Concentrate on the difference between the number of syllables you hear in the singular and plural words.

● Together, try to work out some rules that would help someone who wanted to change another word from singular to plural. What would they need to think about? How important are the sounds, the final letter of the singular word, and the vowel preceding the final letter? (Teachers, see 'Answers' for guidance.)

● Use your discussion to write some spelling guidelines.

NOW TRY THIS

List some words that do not use 's' at all for their plural. What will you put for this group's heading?

ANSWERS

● Most plurals end in 's', and you cannot hear an extra syllable.
● Words ending in 'e' just add 's'.
● You must add 'es' when the singular word ends in a hissing, shushing or buzzing noise. The 'e' is added to make the plural easier to say; otherwise there would be too many 's' sounds.
● If you can hear an extra syllable (for example, 'dish' (one syllable) becomes 'dishes' (two syllables), you know you must add 'es'.
● Words ending in 'y' add 's' if the 'y' is preceded by a vowel. If the 'y' is not preceded by a vowel, the 'y' changes to 'i' and then 'es' is added.

HEAR THOSE MARKS!

OBJECTIVE: to use the apostrophe to spell contracted forms of words
LEARNING LINK: kinaesthetic, visual
ORGANISATION: whole class
RESOURCES: text with numerous contraction apostrophes (such as that in *Reply from Miss Informal*), to be read out

WHAT TO DO

● Talk as a class about the apostrophe. Discuss:
 1. What it looks like;
 2. How it can be used to represent missing letters (for example 'I'll' instead of 'I will').

● A text will be read out to you. Every time you 'hear' an apostrophe, draw the apostrophe shape in the air.

● Keep a record of how many apostrophes you drew. Did you hear all of them?

NOW TRY THIS

Quickly write your own short text containing plenty of contraction apostrophes (or you could use your note from 'Reply from Miss Informal'). Work with a partner, taking turns to read each other your texts. How many apostrophes did you each draw in the air? Did your partner miss any? Award each other an accuracy score.

WHAT'S MY STYLE?

OBJECTIVE: to learn to spell lists of words
LEARNING LINK: visual
ORGANISATION: individual; pairs
RESOURCES: previous week's spelling list or spellings from the children's own log; this activity can be used as a follow-up to 'Doing well!'

WHAT TO DO

● Think about your spelling mistakes. What methods have you used to learn the words that cause you difficulty?
● What about spelling homework? How do you usually tackle it?
● Discuss and compare methods with a partner. Make suggestions that might help each other with your current lists of words to learn.
● Help your partner decide on the best method for their learning: for example, the way a word looks; a spelling rule; pronunciation; oral tests; making up mnemonics. Try out some methods on some of the words in your list.
● Which method do you each prefer?

NOW TRY THIS

Select two words that give you both a spelling problem and try out two methods of learning, a different one for each word. Which method gives you the best results? Which style of learning suits your mind?

WIZARD SHOPPING!

OBJECTIVE: to investigate the effect of adding suffixes to words ending in 'f' and 'fe'
LEARNING LINK: kinaesthetic
ORGANISATION: pairs
RESOURCES: Wilf's shopping list (see below) written on the whiteboard

---

Wilf's shopping list
one spellbook shelf
one sturdy safe
one dog's sniff
one yellow cuff
one magibread loaf
one tall giraffe
one goblin's wife
one magic staff
one green dwarf
one Indian chief
one walnut half

WHAT TO DO

● A sorcerer has dictated a spell shopping list to Wilf, his apprentice. The list is written on the whiteboard.
● Wilf decides to play a trick and order, by phone, lots (plurals) of each 'f' and 'fe' item.
● With a partner, take turns to act out telephoning the order to 'Manic Magicians'. One of you plays the part of Wilf; the other is the shop worker, listening to the order and noticing the pronunciation of the 'fe' and 'f' plurals.
● Discuss plurals that you and your partner disagreed on. 'Eavesdrop' as another pair act out the order. Does this settle your disagreement?

NOW TRY THIS

Present your conversation to the class. Discuss and agree on the correct plural forms.

WHAT AM I?

OBJECTIVE: to explore homonyms
LEARNING LINK: visual
ORGANISATION: individual or pairs
RESOURCES: a list of homonyms double identity clues (see below) to be read out; the answers (in parentheses) written on the whiteboard; a small whiteboard and a marker pen, for each child; this activity can be used as a follow-up to 'Riddle me'

Homonyms
This often sticks to part of my mouth. (gum)
I keep fit by travelling on rails. (train)
Tell the time as you keep a look out. (watch)
Join this society and receive a stick. (club)
Phone me and I'll buy you some jewellery! (ring)
I'm out at night, ready to play rounders. (bat)
Give me a signal from the sea. (wave)
I got up and picked a flower. (rose)
It is not dark when I switch this on. (light)

WHAT TO DO

● Remind yourself of what homonyms are.
● Can you think of any?
● Now play a game of 'What am I?' You will be given a double clue to the identity of a word. You must listen to the clue, choose the correct word from the whiteboard, write it on your individual whiteboard and hold it up. How quickly can you work out the double identity word?

NOW TRY THIS

Compose your own double identity clues. Use them to challenge the rest of the class.

LOOK AND LISTEN

OBJECTIVE: to spell words which differ in pronunciation but have common letter strings
LEARNING LINK: visual
ORGANISATION: pairs; whole class
RESOURCES: word lists (see below) written on the whiteboard

Words

Set 1 pour, shout, yours, mourn, route, four, our, journey, could, out, would

Set 2 bear, learn, fear, dreary, near, earn, wear, heart, gear, dear, hear

WHAT TO DO

● Look at the first set of words on the whiteboard.
● Try to work out what the words have in common (the letter string 'ou').
● There is something strange about this similarity! Can you work out what it is by reading the words aloud to a partner? (They are not all pronounced the same.)
● Share your conclusions with the whole class. How many different pronunciations did you hear?

NOW TRY THIS

Repeat the activity with an investigation of the second set of words on the whiteboard. Can you add more words to the pronunciation groups?

CAN YOU HEAR ME?

OBJECTIVE: to investigate words containing silent letters
LEARNING LINK: visual
ORGANISATION: pairs
RESOURCES: a copy of text containing words with silent letters (see below); a pencil and a dictionary, for each child

Text

King Arthur set the new **k**night his task. 'When the lake is ca**l**m, you must capture a sa**l**mon. **W**rap it in a sack and tie a firm **k**not. Place the bundle at the tom**b** of Sir Lancelot. You should **k**neel there until a **s**word appears in the hand of Lancelot. Take the **k**nife and use it to defeat the monster w**h**ale of the lake.'
'Yes, your Majesty,' answered the **k**night.

WHAT TO DO

● Work with a partner. You should each have a copy of the story.
● Take turns reading the story to each other.
● The listener must be on the alert for letters they cannot hear and underline them on their text.
● Afterwards, compare your results. Have you both underlined the same letters? If there is disagreement, consult a dictionary for advice on pronouncing the disputed words.

NOW TRY THIS

Write a new story containing at least six words with silent letters. Read the text to your partner. Can they spot all of the silent letters?

BUZZ CHALLENGE

OBJECTIVE: to practise spelling new words
LEARNING LINK: kinaesthetic
ORGANISATION: groups of four
RESOURCES: a list of words that the children have heard, read and written recently, perhaps in a science topic

WHAT TO DO

● You are going to play your own version of the television quiz, *University Challenge*.
● Form teams of four. Each team will be questioned in turn. Your team will have one to two minutes to confer; then your chosen representative must answer. If the answer is wrong, or the time is up, someone in another team (no conferring!) may 'buzz', answer and win the point.
● The teacher will spell a word orally. Your team must answer by saying what the word is.
● After a few rounds, the format changes: the teacher will say a word, and your team must say its meaning.
● Make sure everyone in your team has a turn at being the team representative.

NOW TRY THIS

The rounds are getting tougher! Now the teacher will say a word, and your team must respond with its spelling (perhaps with three minutes for conferring, and allowing two or three attempts at the right answer).

READ THIS!

OBJECTIVE: to explore homonyms

LEARNING LINK: kinaesthetic

ORGANISATION: individual; pairs; whole class

RESOURCES: copies of stories written by the children containing 8–10 underlined homonyms, preferably some homonyms with a choice of pronunciation (or use the stories written in 'Radio writer') for each child; this activity can be used as a follow-up to 'Riddle me'

WHAT TO DO

● Swap your story with a partner.

● You are an actor, and you are back at work again in the radio studio. This time you have to broadcast your partner's story to the radio audience.

● Your partner has underlined some words in the story that could be confusing. Be careful how you pronounce them.

● After a quick rehearsal, make your broadcast to your audience.

NOW TRY THIS

In a class discussion, talk about the words underlined in the story you read, why they could be confusing and how you pronounced them.

GOT YOU!

OBJECTIVE: to recognise and spell suffixes and root words

LEARNING LINK: visual

ORGANISATION: pairs

RESOURCES: paper and a pencil for each child; the children could omit the early part of this activity by using their lists from 'All aboard' (this activity can be used as a follow-up)

WHAT TO DO

● Work with a partner to create a chart with four columns.

● Label the columns with these suffixes: 'ship', 'hood', 'ness' and 'ment'.

● Agree on words that end in these suffixes. Aim to write about six to eight per column.

● Talk about the meanings of the words. Check the root words and discuss if and how the new word's meaning has changed by adding a suffix.

● Now discover how much you have learned! Take turns using the list of words: you read out a word; your partner has 30 seconds to say its root word. In ten tries, how many times do you catch your partner out? Now reverse roles.

● After three rounds, who is the 'Got you!' champion?

NOW TRY THIS

Play the game again, this time with 30 seconds to say the root word and spell it orally. Is there a new 'Got you!' champion?

PAST AND PRESENT

OBJECTIVE: to spell the endings of regular verbs

LEARNING LINK: visual

ORGANISATION: individual; pairs or groups

RESOURCES: a story for dictation (see below); verbs from the story listed on the whiteboard (to be revealed at the end of the activity); paper and a pencil, for each child

---

Story

He *was* so greedy, he *grabbed* the lot! For one dinner, he *had* four pieces of plaice in batter; and for dessert, he *ate* a whole cake with a cherry on. Still he *carried* on! Soon he *was slurping* ice cream, and then he *was spied* with his gaze on the sweet jar. Finally, his friends *dragged* him away from the table. They *were saving* everyone else's meal!

WHAT TO DO

● Listen to the story, and see if you can spot the verbs.

● Now listen to the story again. This time it will be read more slowly, so that you will have time to write down the verbs when you hear them.

● Look at the list of verbs on the whiteboard. Did you spot all of them? Did you spell them correctly?

● Discuss any spelling errors with a partner or in a group. Were there any common mistakes? What do many of the verbs have in common? ('ed'; the use of 'was') What does this tell you? (They are in the past tense.)

NOW TRY THIS

When the same story is told in the present tense, what happens to the spelling of the verbs? What are some important spelling changes for verbs when they change tense? Which verbs are particularly 'dangerous'? (verbs ending in 'y')

LISTEN TO THIS!

OBJECTIVE: to use the apostrophe to spell contracted forms of words
LEARNING LINK: visual
ORGANISATION: pairs
RESOURCES: paper and a pencil, for each child

WHAT TO DO

● Work with a partner. Take turns to tell each other about something interesting that you did last night or at the weekend.
● Try to speak naturally, at a normal pace.
● As a listener, make a tally count of every time your partner uses a contraction.
● Afterwards, compare the number of contractions you each heard. Which contraction seems to be the most common in your speech?

NOW TRY THIS

Repeat the investigation of the way you talk by holding a two- to three-minute conversation with your partner and recording it. Then play it back, listening carefully to identify contractions. Listen more than once to make sure you have heard them all. Can you write them down, using apostrophes accurately?

SOUND SEARCHERS

OBJECTIVE: to recognise what happens to words ending in 'f' when 's' is added
LEARNING LINK: visual
ORGANISATION: individual
RESOURCES: text containing words ending in 'fs' and 'ves' (see below), to be read out; two pieces of card and a pen, for each child

Text

Father Christmas *sniffs* unhappily as he looks around his storeroom. The *shelves* are almost bare! All those *roofs* to travel across and so little to put in his sack. He *puffs* out his cheeks and sighs. Then he remembers his *elves*. With their help, he can work wonders! In the next few days, *wolves* and *calves* are made for toy animal sets; *cuffs* are sewn onto football shirts; *scarves* are knitted in fashionable colours; goalkeeping *gloves* are made from leather. On Christmas Eve, Father Christmas travels everywhere as he yet again *saves* the day.

WHAT TO DO

● Make two cards labelled 'fs' and 'ves'.

● Say the words *halves* and *cliffs*. Which sounds softer? ('halves') Which card will match the soft sound? ('ves')
● Now listen to a story which contains several examples of these sounds (see below, left). When you hear one of the sounds, hold up the correct card.
● Listen to the story again, and try to remember the words that you hear which contain these sounds. At the end of the story, the teacher will ask you to list as many as you can.

NOW TRY THIS

In pairs, each write a paragraph using eight to ten plural words ending in 'fs' and 'ves'. Do not let your partner see what you have written! Now take turns to read out each other's stories, the listener holding up the correct 'fs' or 'ves' card when appropriate. Who is the better sound searcher?

PRONUNCIATION PRACTICE

OBJECTIVE: to spell words which differ in pronunciation but have common letter strings
LEARNING LINK: tactile, visual
ORGANISATION: pairs
RESOURCES: a word list (see below) and a pencil for each child; a dictionary for each pair; this activity can be used as a follow-up to 'Wordsearch'

Words

bough, cough, bought, rough, though, enough, nought, although, dough, plough, sought, through, tough, trough, thought

WHAT TO DO

● Work with a partner. Each of you will be given a list of words containing 'ough'.
● Listen as your partner says the words. Put a tick by the words on your list if you agree with your partner's pronunciation. Put a cross if you disagree.
● Now reverse roles: you read aloud, while your partner puts ticks or crosses on their list.
● Compare results. Discuss any words that you or your partner have put a cross beside. Use a dictionary to help you reach agreement on the correct pronunciation.

NOW TRY THIS

Discuss your results with a partner. Put the words into pronunciation groups. Can you find a rhyming pair or set? How many different pronunciations have you found? Label the groups to help you remember the pronunciation.

HEAR WHAT YOU SEE

OBJECTIVE: to aid the spelling of compound words when pronunciation obscures it
LEARNING LINK: visual
ORGANISATION: pairs
RESOURCES: a word list (see below) and a pencil, for each child

---

Compound words

cupboard, handkerchief, grandchild, raspberry, outside, football, postman, grandmother, windmill, goodnight

---

WHAT TO DO

- Work with a partner. Each of you will be given a list of words.
- Take turns being the speaker.
- The speaker reads out each word in turn. The listener puts a circle around the silent letter (the one that they do not hear in the pronunciation of the word). Do not let your partner see what letters you have circled.
- When you have both had an opportunity to be the listener, compare your results. Did you both find the same letter easily missed?

NOW TRY THIS

Discuss ways to remember each spelling, including the silent letter. What tips do you have? Does it help to think of the word in two parts?

SOUNDS RIGHT?

OBJECTIVE: to investigate words ending in 'a', 'i', 'o' and 'u'
LEARNING LINK: visual
ORGANISATION: individual; pairs
RESOURCES: a word list (see below) for each child; this activity can be used as a follow-up to 'Strangely similar!'

Words

ravioli, piccolo, emu, panda, armadillo, concerto, risotto, chapatti, bureau, banjo, tagliatelli, tarantula, viola, oratorio, spaghetti, gecko, magnolia, gala, broccoli, igloo, antenna, piano, camera, tomato, potato, scampi, ski, gnu, tutu, tableau, kimono, haiku

---

WHAT TO DO

- Read through the list of words. Try saying them aloud. Do you notice anything strange about their endings? (They all end in a vowel.)

- Work with your partner, taking turns saying the words to each other. The listener must reply with what they think is the plural form. Watch out! There are some that do not change.
- Make sure that you both have a turn at supplying the plural for every word.
- Think about where you gave different replies. Highlight those words on your lists.
- Try saying your replies again. Which plural sounds right? Can you now reach agreement?

NOW TRY THIS

Write the plurals and sort the original list into groups according to how the words form their plurals. How many groups do you need? Compare results as a class.

SILLY MNEMONICS

OBJECTIVE: to identify misspellings and learn to spell them correctly
LEARNING LINK: visual
ORGANISATION: individuals; small groups
RESOURCES: mnemonics for some common spelling problems (see below); a small whiteboard and a marker pen, for each child

---

Mnemonics

tear: Tom's Elbows Are Ripped
lamb: Larry Ate Meat Balls
fruit: Fleas Race Up Inside Trousers
heard: His Ears Are Rather Droopy
because: Big Elephants Can Always Understand Small Elephants
beautiful: Bugs Eat Ants Up Trees, In Flowers, Under Leaves
rhythm: Rhythm Helps Your Two Hips Move

WHAT TO DO

- Have you noticed how the same old spelling mistakes keep cropping up over and over again? Here is a brilliant way to help you remember these spellings: silly mnemonics!
- Remind yourself of what a mnemonic is (for example, 'hippos always like floods' = 'half').
- The teacher will call out some mnemonics. Your job is to identify the word! Write and display the answers on your individual whiteboard.
- In small groups, make up some mnemonics of your own.

NOW TRY THIS

Working with a partner, identify a word from recent writing that has given you both a spelling problem and create a mnemonic for it.

CATCH THAT JINGLE

OBJECTIVE: to investigate rules for regular spellings
LEARNING LINK: kinaesthetic, visual
ORGANISATION: pairs or small groups
RESOURCES: singular and plural noun pairs written on the whiteboard (see below); paper and a pencil, for each child

Singular and plural forms
lorry/lorries; city/cities; bus/buses; watch/watches; monkey/monkeys; toy/toys

WHAT TO DO
● Look at the pairs of words on the whiteboard. Discuss how the plurals have been formed, talk about the differences and the possible spelling traps.
● Work out some spelling rules. Which is the one you really want to stick in your mind?
● Pretend that you are in Australia! You work for School of the Air, transmitting radio programmes to children who live in remote areas of the country. You need a catchy jingle that will help your listeners remember one or more of these rules.
● With your partner or group, decide which rule(s) to work on, for at least one jingle.

NOW TRY THIS
Rehearse by saying, chanting or singing your jingle before you make the radio transmission to the rest of the class. Which jingle (and therefore spelling rule) sticks in your brain most easily?

SPELLING BEE

OBJECTIVE: to identify word roots, derivations and spelling patterns
LEARNING LINK: visual
ORGANISATION: individual; pairs
RESOURCES: sentence and list of root words (see below) written on the whiteboard; paper and a pencil, for each child; this activity can be used as a follow-up to 'From little roots 1'

Sentence
The hero was praised for his heroism after the heroic act.
Word roots
prove, pass, public, give, hand, obey, examine, pain, relate, call, cover

WHAT TO DO
● Look at the sentence on the whiteboard, and identify the three connected words ('hero', 'heroism', 'heroic'). What is the word root? ('hero')
● Now look at the list of word roots on the whiteboard.
● Choose six of these word roots. Make up and write a sentence for each one, using the word root and one or two associated words linked by spelling and meaning. (Alternatively, you could use your sentences from *From little roots 1*.) Remember that the root may be contained inside the new word: for example, 'discovery' is derived from the word root 'cover'.
● When the teacher has checked your work, take turns in reading your sentences to a partner. Can the listener quickly identify the root word and its associates?

NOW TRY THIS
Repeat the activity, but this time the listener should say the answers and spell them orally. Award a point for each correct spelling.

COLLECTING POINTS

OBJECTIVE: to recognise and spell suffixes
LEARNING LINK: visual
ORGANISATION: small groups
RESOURCES: postbox drawn on the whiteboard labelled with one of the following suffixes: 'ible', 'able', 'ic', 'al'; paper and a pencil, for each group

WHAT TO DO
● Get into small teams. To collect points for your team, you need to post words orally in the postbox on the whiteboard.
● Look at the label on the postbox. It is only open for collections of words ending in that suffix.
● The teams take it in turns to suggest words for the postbox. One point is awarded for a correct word, and a second point for its correct pronunciation.
● As the game proceeds, the teacher writes the collected words on the postbox.
● Each team keeps a record of their own points.
● When the box closes, add up your points to see which team has the highest score.
● Can you think of any words you missed?

NOW TRY THIS
Repeat the game using a postbox with a different suffix label. This time, there is an extra point available for correct oral spelling.

FULL OF TROUBLE!

OBJECTIVE: to explore and establish rules for patterns of consonants
LEARNING LINK: visual
ORGANISATION: pairs; individual
RESOURCES: list of words to be extended (see below) written on the whiteboard; a dictionary, paper and a pencil, for each child

Words
play, plenty, harm, mercy, thank, boast, hope, pity, doubt, fear, faith

WHAT TO DO

● The teacher will read out three words to you ('beautiful', 'careful' and 'colourful').
● What do these words mean? What word can you hear at the end of each? How does it affect the meaning of the first word? (Nouns and verbs become adjectives; adjectives stay as adjectives.)
● Look at the list of words on the whiteboard. Read them aloud to a partner, taking turns to add the word 'full' orally. You need to consider:
   1. Does the new, longer word sound right?
   2. What does it mean?
● Write down the new words that you said. Do they look strange? Why?
● Check the spellings in a dictionary. What do you find out?
● Using what you have learned, try to spell 'beautiful, careful' and 'colourful'.

NOW TRY THIS

1. Compose a clear explanation of what happens to 'full' when it is used as a suffix.
2. As a class, design a classroom poster to reinforce this spelling rule (for example, one 'l' could fall down as 'full' joins a word).

HARD OR SOFT CANDY?

OBJECTIVE: to explore spelling patterns using the consonant 'c' and formulate rules
LEARNING LINK: visual
ORGANISATION: pairs
RESOURCES: two word lists (see below) written on the whiteboard; paper and a pencil, for each child

Words
List A: cinema, cold, except, celebrity, cupboard, cube, decimal, recover, circle, calendar
List B: coat, cereal, cat, decide, curtain, camera, December, recite, column, carnival

WHAT TO DO

● Work with a partner. One of you should copy down list A from the whiteboard, while the other copies list B.
● Prepare a listening sheet: on a new piece of paper, each of you should make a blank list, numbered from one to ten.
● One partner reads the list A words aloud, one by one, as the other partner listens and decides if they have heard a hard or a soft 'c' sound. On their listening sheet, the listener should enter an appropriate 'h' (hard) or 's' (soft) for each number.
● Now swap roles, with the other partner reading list B.
● Make another listening sheet. Exchange word lists and repeat the experiment, but this time each listening to the other word list.
● Finally, compare listening results. Did you always hear the same hard or soft sound? If you disagree, you need to investigate further (perhaps using a dictionary).

NOW TRY THIS

Investigate the link between spelling and the pronunciation of 'c'. What can you discover? How relevant is the vowel following 'c'? Try to work out a rule. Do any of the words in the lists break the rule?

NOW TRY THIS

NOW TRY THIS

Analyse your charts. Which is the most common pronunciation? Can you add your own 'ear' words to the columns?

> **ANSWERS**
> **A:** ear, fear, gear, beard, clear, year, tear
> **B:** pear, wear, bear, tear
> **C:** yearn, earth, search, learn
> **D:** heart, hearth

-EAR, -EAR!

OBJECTIVE: to investigate words which differ in pronunciation but have common letter strings
LEARNING LINK: visual
ORGANISATION: pairs
RESOURCES: word list (see below) and a pencil, for each child

> **Word list**
> ear, fear, pear, yearn, tear (1), earth, gear, wear, beard, search, heart, clear, tear (2), learn, hearth, year, bear

WHAT TO DO

● Make yourself a listening chart with four columns. Label the first column 'A'.

● Look at the photocopied list of words, all containing the 'ear' letter string. Notice that 'tear' is written twice, but with different meanings (the water that drips from your eye; a rip).

● Work with a partner. Say the word *ear* aloud to each other. Listen carefully to its sound, and write the word in column A. Tick the word on your list. Read it aloud again. Remember that it is the sound you are listening for!

● Read aloud all the words on the list to each other, ticking and writing a word in column A every time it makes the sound you are listening for. Do this more than once until you are sure you have identified all the words that belong in column A.

● Look at the words you have not ticked. Read one of them aloud, listening carefully to the sound made by its 'ear' letter string. Tick the word and write it in column B. Read aloud the other unticked words, listening for others to add to B.

● Continue your investigation with other columns until all the words are placed. How many columns did you need? How many different ways have you found to pronounce the 'ear' letter string?

ATTEN-SHUN!

OBJECTIVE: to recognise and spell a common group of suffixes
LEARNING LINK: visual
ORGANISATION: individual
RESOURCES: a dictionary, paper and a pencil, for each child

WHAT TO DO

● Travel back in time to your Reception class! You cannot spell well, but you do know how sounds are made.

● Listen while the teacher says the word *attention*.

● Concentrate on the last syllable of the word. As a pupil in a Reception class, how would you spell this syllable phonetically? ('shun')

● Think of 10–15 words that also end in a 'shun' sound. Make quick, written recordings of the words' beginnings only (for example, 'frac').

● Now you are back in the present day! Do you know the correct spelling of the final syllable of 'attention'? ('tion')

NOW TRY THIS

Work with a partner, saying your lists of words to each other. How many ways can you find to spell this ending? Use dictionaries to put the words into groups (for example, 'cian', 'sion'). Compare your results with the rest of the class.

BET YOU MISS ME!

OBJECTIVE: to spell words with unstressed vowels
LEARNING LINK: visual
ORGANISATION: small groups; whole class
RESOURCES: a list of words to be read aloud (see below) and then displayed in two stages; this activity can be used as a follow-up to 'Father Christmas's helper'

Words
Stage 1: literacy, monastery, dictionary
Stage 2: frightening, general, preparatory, heaven, easily, carpet, deafening, Wednesday, library, imaginary, animal, generous, lottery, business, formal, miserable, jewellery

WHAT TO DO
● The teacher will read a selection of words to you (from both lists). Close your eyes and try to visualise what you hear.
● Now look at the Stage 1 words on the whiteboard while they are read aloud to you. Does what you hear match what you see?
● In small groups, discuss any spelling difficulties. Is there a specific problem? Does one particular type of letter keep giving a problem?
● Share views as a class. What is causing the spelling problem? (unstressed vowels)

NOW TRY THIS
Look at the Stage 2 words. Work in pairs, taking it in turns to say the words or listen. Identify the 'dangerous' unstressed vowel in each word.

MAGIC E

OBJECTIVE: to investigate the use of a modifying 'e'
LEARNING LINK: visual
ORGANISATION: pairs
RESOURCES: a word list (see below) for each pair; this activity can be used as a follow-up to 'Archaeological dig'

Base words
care, love, shame, live, hope, rehearse, sure, use, tune, pave, hate

WHAT TO DO
● Work with a partner, taking turns to read to each other the list of base words. Then look carefully at them together.

● What do you notice about the spelling of the base words?
● Make sure that you have both spotted the final 'e'.
● Again take turns saying the words to each other. Try saying the words (if it is possible) without the final 'e'; then again with the 'e'. Can you work out the sound effect caused by the 'e'? Which other letter's sound is affected?
● What have you found out that will help you with your spelling?

NOW TRY THIS
Make an oral report of your findings to the class. Discuss as a class whether knowing how to say a word helps you spell it.

SAY NO!

OBJECTIVE: to recognise the spelling and meaning of prefixes
LEARNING LINK: visual
ORGANISATION: pairs
RESOURCES: a word list (see below) for each child; this activity can be used as a follow-up to 'Negative thinking' and 'Give and take'

Words
irresponsible, incorrect, illegal, improper, improbable, illegible, irregular, inactive, illiterate, impossible

WHAT TO DO
● Work with a partner, reading together the list of words. Remind yourselves how to pronounce the words and what they mean. You should notice something about their meanings and how each word begins.
● Take turns at choosing a word from the list and getting your partner to guess which word you have chosen. Give your partner a spelling or mnemonic clue that is not too obvious. For example, 'illegible': it has sick at the beginning ('ill'); 'impossible': it starts with a naughty person ('imp').
● Challenge your partner to identify the word, and award a point for each correct answer (perhaps with a time limit, to keep the game moving quickly).

NOW TRY THIS
Give mnemonic clues to words of your own that also begin with a negative prefix. (You could use your list from 'Now try this' in *Give and take*.)

EASY LISTENING

OBJECTIVE: to identify spelling mistakes in own writing and learn to correct them
LEARNING LINK: visual
ORGANISATION: groups; individual
RESOURCES: facilities for audio recording (part of the day or literacy lesson could be dedicated to group listening to the spelling recording)

WHAT TO DO

● Solve your spelling difficulties with some brainwashing!
● In groups, identify five to ten spellings that cause particular difficulty for each of you. Try to find some that the whole group has in common.
● Make an audio recording, each of you saying your words, and spelling them aloud letter by letter.
● Listen to your part of the tape in spare moments, aiming at once a day.

NOW TRY THIS

After two weeks, ask a partner to test you. Are your spelling problems disappearing?

DINING FOR DINNER

OBJECTIVE: to spell words of two syllables which contain a double consonant
LEARNING LINK: visual
ORGANISATION: pairs
RESOURCES: a word list (see below); two cards numbered 1 and 2 for each pair; the following sentence written on the whiteboard: 'The diner ate his dinner in a smart restaurant.'

Words
coma, comma; hoping, hopping; supper, super; taping, tapping; bitter, biter; dinner, diner; loping, lopping; writing, written; caring, carry

---

WHAT TO DO

● Look at the sentence on the whiteboard. Which two words look almost the same? What is the difference in meaning? Is pronunciation important?
● Discuss with a partner how a student learning English would know how to pronounce those two words differently. What is the effect of doubling the consonant 'n'?
● One of you will be given a card with '1' on it, and the other a card with '2' on it. The teacher will call out words that contain either a single or double consonant. You and your partner must decide which of you needs to hold up your number.

● Play the game again. This time, identify which consonant is being used, as well as the number.

NOW TRY THIS

Play the game in reverse! When the teacher calls out the number and identity of the consonant to be used, write an appropriate word on your individual whiteboard.

INTERPRETER NEEDED!

OBJECTIVE: to investigate words with common letter strings
LEARNING LINK: visual
ORGANISATION: pairs or groups of three; whole class
RESOURCES: audio recording containing confused speech, including some words with common letter strings (see below); paper and a pencil, for each child

---

Suggested examples of confused speech
Chop statting. (Stop chatting.)
Dit sown. (Sit down.)
Bet your gooks. (Get your books.)
Han you cear? (Can you hear?)
Ge bood! (Be good!)
Lestin! (Listen!)
Open bour yooks. (Open your books.)
Kool at nage pen. (Look at page ten.)
Cat wholour is it? (What colour is it?)
I can't erndustand. (I can't understand.)
This is no doog. (This is no good.)
KOOL! (Look!)

WHAT TO DO

● Today your teacher's speech is going to be scrambled! Hopefully when it happens, you will still be able to work out what they mean.
● Get into pairs or groups of three. Listen to an audio recording of the scrambled speech. You have one minute to think about how to unscramble it, and then your group will have to present their translation!
● Afterwards, the teacher will write some of the scrambled sentences on the board, so you can examine them more closely. Which letter strings have been involved? Which sounds have changed places?

NOW TRY THIS

Working in pairs, give your partner a short instruction. Can the listener turn those words into gibberish with scrambled sounds? Try the same thing in reverse.

LISTEN AND TELL

OBJECTIVE: to use the endings 'f', 'ff' and 'fe'

LEARNING LINK: visual

ORGANISATION: individual

RESOURCES: a word list (see below); a dictionary, paper and a pencil, for each child; this activity can be used as a follow-up to 'Race the clock' or an introduction to 'Scarfs and scarves'

Words

cliff, loaf, wolf, knife, chief, staff, elf, huff

WHAT TO DO

● You are going to hear some singular words ending in 'f', 'ff' or 'fe' being read aloud.

● As you listen to each word, make an oral prediction of its ending. Now the teacher will reveal the correct version. How many did you get right?

● Try again, and see if you can improve your success rate.

● Make a list of at least ten other singular words with these endings. Say them to yourself, and then write them as you think they are spelled. When you have finished, check your spelling in a dictionary and work out your success rate.

NOW TRY THIS

Try out your word list (or you could use your list from 'Race the clock') on a partner, using the same oral prediction format. How good is your partner at predicting the ending of each word on your list?

SCARFS AND SCARVES

OBJECTIVE: to investigate words ending in 'f', 'ff' and 'fe' and their plurals

LEARNING LINK: visual

ORGANISATION: pairs; whole class

RESOURCES: a word list (see below), paper and a pencil for each child; this activity can be used as a follow-up to 'Race the clock' and 'Listen and tell'

Singular and plural words

cliff/cliffs; staff/staffs; huff/huffs; sniff/sniffs; cuff/cuffs; puff/puffs;

loaf/loaves; wolf/wolves; chief/chiefs; elf/elves; belief/beliefs; half/halves; scarf/scarves; shelf/shelves; wife/wives; knife/knives; life/lives

---

WHAT TO DO

● In pairs, put together a joint collection of singular words ending in 'f', 'ff' and 'fe'.

● As a whole class, agree on a selection of about 15–20 words for each ending. Which ending was hardest to collect for?

● Now the teacher will call out the singular form of some words with these endings (for example, *wife*) and will select a pair of children to say the plural (*wives*), pronouncing it correctly. You can win an extra point by spelling the plural correctly.

NOW TRY THIS

With your partner, try playing the game backwards: one partner says the plural form, and the other has 30 seconds to say and write the correct singular form.

GIVE US A CLUE

OBJECTIVE: to use analogy with other known words as a spelling aid

LEARNING LINK: kinaesthetic

ORGANISATION: individual; groups

RESOURCES: recent homework spelling lists; paper and a pencil, for each child

WHAT TO DO

● Think of three words from your two last homework spelling lists. Keep them secret from the rest of the class, and check their spelling.

● For each word, make up two spelling clues and one meaning clue. For example, for the word 'brief', the clues could be:

  1. I have an 'ee' sound;

  2. But I use the 'ie' letter string;

  3. My meaning does not last long.

● Play the game in groups, taking turns at giving clues. When it is your turn, give your clues one at a time, pausing to allow two guesses at your identity. Three points are awarded for guessing correctly after the first clue, two points after the second clue and if the final meaning clue is given, only one point is scored.

● If the listeners cannot guess the word in three attempts, then the clue-giver reveals the word and steals the point.

NOW TRY THIS

Play the game again using words from a different source (for example, words from a classroom display). Set a time limit for making guesses.

TACTILE LEARNING

TOUCH AND TELL

OBJECTIVE: to investigate the spelling pattern 'le'
LEARNING LINK: kinaesthetic, visual
ORGANISATION: pairs
RESOURCES: large separate lower case letters 'l' and 'e' cut out from stiff card and a copy of the text (see below); card, pencils and scissors, for each pair

Text
What a relief! At last, the muddle was over: the plant's prickle had done its work and each bubble had burst. It would be a long time before those unreliable letters were able to work their mischief again! However, more trouble was on the way. Soon there was a giggle from the alphabet box, a cackle from the word sack and…

WHAT TO DO
● Join up with a partner. Close your eyes, as your partner hands you a letter card. Can you identify it by feel? Swap over, making ten attempts each and keep a record of your success.
● Discuss the game. Was it easy? How did you make your identifications?
● Study the text and find three words ending in 'le', but that have a double letter just before. Choose four words, each with a different letter preceding 'le' and both of you make those four letters in card.
● Play 'Touch and tell' again, this time with the new letters. Again, have ten tries each.
● Now compare your success. Discuss how you decided your answers. Did you notice something special about the shape of most of the letters? (They all have ascenders and descenders.) If not, play the game again, concentrating on finding a link.

NOW TRY THIS
Extend your investigation to a chapter of your reading book and a dictionary, finding words that use a double letter before 'le'. List the letters before 'le'. How many fit the pattern you discovered earlier? Which ones do not have an ascender or descender?

MAKING WINNERS

OBJECTIVE: to recognise how the addition of 'ing' changes the spelling of verbs
LEARNING LINK: auditory, visual
ORGANISATION: pairs
RESOURCES: base words (see below) written on the whiteboard; pencils and a generous supply of blank word cards or paper, for each child

Base words
come, do, chat, stare, enjoy, smile, meet, cut, amaze, take, tack, shape, shop, slide, ask, rid, tip, tape, pull, hope, drive, hop, win, jump

WHAT TO DO
● Working in pairs, write the base words on word cards. Put the cards face down in a pile.
● Take turns turning over and reading aloud a base word. As the reader, try to win the word for your personal winners' enclosure. All you have to do is add 'ing' (on a blank card) and place it beside the word. For example, for 'stop' or 'race' you may write '+ ing'. If your partner agrees with the new word made, the complete word moves to your winners' enclosure.
● The catch comes when a spelling change is needed! If, for example, you forget that '+ ping' is needed to make 'stopping', or that an 'e' must be removed to make 'racing' and your partner notices your error, they can reject your answer. In this case, the base word goes to the bottom of the pile.
● Keep playing until all the base words have moved to a winners' enclosure.
● Ask someone to judge your winners.
● Are errors spotted and disqualified?

NOW TRY THIS
Play again with different base words.

ANSWERS
come – coming; do – doing; chat – chatting; stare – staring; enjoy – enjoying; smile – smiling; meet – meeting; cut – cutting; amaze – amazing; take – taking; tack – tacking; shape – shaping; shop – shopping; slide – sliding; ask – asking; rid – ridding; tip – tipping; tape – taping; pull – pulling; hope – hoping; drive – driving; hop – hopping; win – winning; jump – jumping

REMEMBER THAT PLACE

OBJECTIVE: to spell common prefixes and recognise how they influence word meanings
LEARNING LINK: visual
ORGANISATION: pairs
RESOURCES: a word list (see below) written on the whiteboard; 20 blank word cards and scissors, for each pair

Words

displease, incorrect, unable, impossible, disagree, misplace, inconvenient, misbehave, impolite, disobey, invisible, mis-spell, imperfect, dishonest, disqualify, misunderstand, improbable, informal, immature, mislead

WHAT TO DO

● With a partner, make a total of 20 word cards using the words listed above.
● Cut the prefix away from the base word so that you end up with 40 cards. Shuffle the cards and spread them out face down in front of you.
● Now you are going to play a game of 'Remember that place' to improve your memory and word-building skills. You and your partner should take turns to turn over two cards. If these cards make a word, both cards are claimed as a prize. If the cards do not link up, they are returned to their places face down.

NOW TRY THIS

Play this as a class activity on the interactive whiteboard, using a screen of cards, each with a prefix or base word. The screen of cards is displayed 'face down' (base words and prefixes are merely concealed). Partners can collaborate to take turns deciding on two cards to turn over. The writing should be revealed, and then concealed again if it does not make a word. Completed words should be dragged to the side.

SNAP!

OBJECTIVE: to investigate rules for adding 's'
LEARNING LINK: kinaesthetic, visual
ORGANISATION: groups of three
RESOURCES: a set of singular word cards (see below), a score sheet, a plural answer sheet (see below) and a pencil, for each group

Singular words
brush, diary, taxi, buoy, tune, pastry, wish, school, play, donkey, melody, ditch, jelly, pond, way, bean, turkey, ruby, tax, dish
Plural answers
s: taxis, tunes, schools, ponds, beans
es: wishes, dishes, taxes, brushes, ditches
ys: buoys, plays, ways, turkeys, donkeys
ies: diaries, melodies, jellies, pastries, rubies

WHAT TO DO

● Form a group of three, choosing one of you to be the dealer.
● As dealer, you will be given a set of singular word cards, a score sheet and a plural answer sheet. (Do not show this to the rest of your group!) Shuffle and deal ten cards to each of the two players, piling their cards face down in front of them.
● The two players take turns at turning over the top card, keeping their eyes peeled for two top cards belonging to the same plural group. The first player to say *Snap!* wins a point, with a bonus point given for a clear explanation of the spelling rule. (The dealer awards points.)
● After two minutes, the dealer collects the cards not won, re-shuffles and deals them so that the game can continue. Remember to keep a record of the palyers' scores.
● After another two minutes, the game is over. Who had the highest score?
● Change roles and play the whole game, with all 20 cards, again. Repeat so that everyone in the group has a chance to be the dealer.

NOW TRY THIS

Collect and shuffle the 20 cards. Spread them out face up and work together to sort them into plural groups. Write a label for each section, explaining its spelling rule.

KNIGHTS AND GNOMES

OBJECTIVE: to investigate and spell words containing silent letters
LEARNING LINK: auditory, kinaesthetic, visual
ORGANISATION: pairs; whole class
RESOURCES: a word list (see below) to be read out; two blank cards, paper and pens, for each pair

Words
Set 1: knuckle, gnome, kneel, knot, gnaw, gnat, knight, knit, knife, gnash, knowledge, knack, gnarled, knoll
Set 2: wretch, rhubarb, wrapper, rhomboid, writer, rhinoceros, wreath, wrinkle, rhapsody, rheumatism, wrist, wrestle, rhyme, rhythm

WHAT TO DO
● With a partner, make two cards: 'kn' and 'gn'.
● Listen while the teacher reads out a list of words (Set 1). Try to visualise each word's starting letters: 'kn' or 'gn'.
● Quickly and quietly, discuss with your partner which card to hold up for each word.
● When everyone has displayed their answers, the correct form will be written on the whiteboard. Keep a record of how many you get right.
● How good were you at telling knights from gnomes? Why could you describe them both as 'sneaky'? (They both begin with a silent letter.)
● Play again to see if your score improves.

NOW TRY THIS
Make new cards for 'wr' and 'rh', and play the game again (this time using the Set 2 words). Which letter is silent in the 'rh' words? ('h')

CAST YOUR VOTE

OBJECTIVE: to investigate, spell and read words containing silent letters
LEARNING LINK: auditory, kinaesthetic, visual
ORGANISATION: individual
RESOURCES: a list of correctly and incorrectly spelled words (see below); two blank cards and pens, for each child

Words
A rino, B rhino
A ryme, B rhyme
A calm, B carm
A wirl, B whirl
A rythm, B rhythm

WHAT TO DO
● Use your blank cards to make two voting cards labelled 'A' and 'B'.
● You will be given two different options for spelling some words, but only one of the options is correct. You must decide which one is right and vote accordingly.
● The teacher will say each word aloud and display its two forms on the whiteboard. After a minute, cast your vote for the correct spelling by holding up the correct card.
● Keep a mental score of your success. How well did you do?
● Try to improve your score by playing the game again.

NOW TRY THIS
Look at the incorrectly spelled words in the list. Can you suggest why these mistakes occurred? (The words contain silent letters.) Think of some other words that contain silent letters.

JOG MY MEMORY!

OBJECTIVE: to explore patterns of consonants
LEARNING LINK: auditory, visual
ORGANISATION: pairs; individual
RESOURCES: a dictionary, a pen, some paper and two blank word cards, for each child

WHAT TO DO
● Write a list of 20 words containing the letter 'c' followed by a vowel. Use a dictionary to help you come up with ideas and to check the spelling.
● Now say the words aloud. Does the 'c' sound hard or soft? Put a special mark beside the words to remind you. Make sure you have some of each type.
● Check your answers with a partner.
● Give other members of your class a helping hand with their 'c' spelling and pronunciation by designing and making two helpful cards.
● Make sure the card is visually memorable, so link the appearance of the word with its sound (for example, an angry face on the hard 'c'). Try to link your example word to its sound (for example, *'cu* in *cut* is hard to get through!').

NOW TRY THIS
In a group of four, use your cards to create hard and soft 'c' posters. Display the posters around the classroom and, as a whole class, vote for the posters which are the most memorable.

JUST A MINUTE!

OBJECTIVE: to recognise and create compound words

LEARNING LINK: auditory, kinaesthetic, visual

ORGANISATION: pairs or groups of three

RESOURCES: a set of word cards (see below), paper and pencils, for each group

Words

every, some, sun, eye, one, light, rain, air, day, fly, berry, cup, black

WHAT TO DO

- Play this game in pairs or groups of three. Write your names on a results sheet.
- You will be given a set of word cards. Pile the cards, face down, in the middle.
- Take turns turning over the top card. When it is your turn, you have one minute to win a point by saying a compound word that uses that word as its start or end.
- If successful, keep the card. If unsuccessful, return the card face down to the bottom of the pile, and let the game move on to the next person.
- Keep a record of your scores and the words made.
- Keep going until all the cards are used. Now tot up the scores.

NOW TRY THIS

Shuffle the cards for another round of the game, in which only new compound words count.

IT'S A MATCH!

OBJECTIVE: to use the apostrophe to spell contracted forms of words

LEARNING LINK: kinaesthetic, visual

ORGANISATION: pairs or groups of three

RESOURCES: photocopiable page 63 containing full word forms and contractions (see below) for each group; glue, card and scissors for each group

Full forms for 12 boxes

do not; I am; will not; there has; I have; cannot; you would; you have; he will; she would; does not; it will

Contractions for 12 boxes

I'm; you've; she'd; it'll; don't; you'd; he'll; there's; doesn't; won't; I've; can't

WHAT TO DO

- Play this game in pairs or groups of three. Each group will receive a sheet of paper with 24 squares. Stick the sheet onto card and cut it up to create a set of 24 cards.
- One group member should shuffle the cards and spread them out face down on the table.
- Take turns at turning over two cards. If, on their turn, a player recognises a link between the cards and calls *It's a match!* they win both cards. Otherwise the cards are returned face down to their original places and the game moves on to the next player.
- Remember, you have to look as well as think! You need to remember where you saw what.

NOW TRY THIS

Make a new set of cards, exchange them with another group, and play the game again.

THAT'S MY NAME!

OBJECTIVE: to use short words contained in longer words as a spelling aid

LEARNING LINK: visual

ORGANISATION: individual

RESOURCES: a small piece of card and colouring pencils or felt-tipped pens for each child; this activity can be used as a follow-up to 'Hidden secrets'

WHAT TO DO

- Do you remember that longer words may contain hidden secrets?
- For example, think about the surname 'Carpenter'. This contains a number of hidden words, such as 'car', 'carp', 'pen', 'pent' and 'enter'.
- At large business meetings, attendees often wear name badges. For fun, and to remind others how to spell his name, Mr Carpenter's badge could also have a pen drawn on it containing the word 'pen'.
- Make a memorable name badge for yourself, a family member or a character from a book, or a classroom pet, mascot or toy.
- The wearer of the badge wants the badge to help others to spell their name. The badge needs to have strong visual impact with a pictorial element that draws attention to a secret word inside.

NOW TRY THIS

Hold an impromptu get-together! Move around the room holding or wearing your badge. Which names do the attendees find most memorable?

TAKE YOUR PICK

OBJECTIVE: to distinguish between different spellings and meanings of homophones
LEARNING LINK: auditory, visual
ORGANISATION: pairs
RESOURCES: homophones and example from *Riddle me*; paper, pencils and felt-tipped pens, for each pair; this activity can be used as a follow-up to 'Riddle me' and 'What am I?'

WHAT TO DO
● Can you remember what 'homophones' are? (Words that have the same sound as another, but a different meaning or spelling.)
● If possible, use your riddles from *Riddle me*. Otherwise, work with a partner to make up some single or double riddles (see page 10).
● You are going to help the teacher with their work, by making some worksheets.
● Share your riddles with a partner, so that you can each create a worksheet with a selection of crafty riddles and choices of answers on the front, and the correct solutions on the back. The answer choices could be presented pictorially.

NOW TRY THIS
Have a trial run of each other's worksheets. Do the riddles make sense? Can you work them out?

JIGSAW DOMINOES

OBJECTIVE: to know the meanings of prefixes
LEARNING LINK: kinaesthetic, visual
ORGANISATION: individual
RESOURCES: a list of prefixes and their meanings (see below) written on the whiteboard; card, pencil and scissors, for each child

---

Prefixes and meanings
De – undo; in – not; un – not; ex – out of; contra – against; tri – three; ab – away from; sub –under; inter – between; non – not; pre – before; re – again; anti – against; bi – two

---

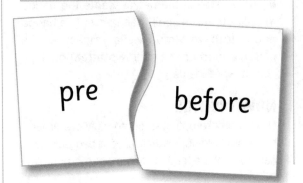

WHAT TO DO
● Make your own domino pieces out of card. Make eight pieces and divide each one with a central line. However, make your central lines vary in shape like jigsaw piece joins: they go in and out.
● Choose eight prefixes from the list on the whiteboard. In one half of each domino, write a prefix; in the other, write its meaning.
● Cut out your domino halves carefully, so that you have 16 separate pieces.
● Jumble them up and try fitting the jigsaws together. How quickly can you manage it?

NOW TRY THIS
Challenge a partner to complete your jigsaws. List each other's prefixes and meanings and discuss the results. Can you think of a word starting with each prefix?

ALPHABET MUDDLE

OBJECTIVE: to explore homonyms with the same spelling but multiple meanings
LEARNING LINK: auditory, kinaesthetic, visual
ORGANISATION: small groups
RESOURCES: sets of homonyms (see below), one set for each group; a dictionary, paper and colouring pencils or felt-tipped pens, for each group

---

Homonyms
Set 1: ape, bat, crane, dash, express
Set 2: flat, gum, hip, iron, jam
Set 3: keep, light, mail, needle, order
Set 4: pound, quick, rush, sole, train
Set 5: uniform, view, watch, yard, zoom

WHAT TO DO
● You are going to contribute to a pictorial, alphabetical homonym display.
● Form a small group. Each group will receive a different set of homonyms.
● Discuss the words within your group, checking that you know the different meanings. Use dictionaries when needed.
● Now draw a picture which illustrates the different meanings of each word. Each picture must show at least two meanings of a word. Divide up the work among the members of your group.

NOW TRY THIS
As a whole class, create a temporary alphabetical display of your pictures on the floor or a table.

MYSTERY PARTNERS

OBJECTIVE: to explore homonyms and homophones
LEARNING LINK: auditory, kinaesthetic, visual
ORGANISATION: pairs
RESOURCES: list of homonyms and homophones (see below), two labels with 'S' and 'D' written on them, card, scissors, glue and a dictionary, for each pair; rules written on the whiteboard (see below)

Words
you, fit, league, might, morning, foot, in, wave, hair, arms, right, heard, him, jam, tug, bye, scuttle, rain, race, leaves

Rules
The homonym cards sound and are spelled the same as their mystery partner, but are different in meaning.
The homophone cards sound the same as their mystery partner, but are different in spelling and meaning.

WHAT TO DO

● Work with a partner. You will be given a sheet of 20 words. Stick these on to card and cut them into word cards.

● Shuffle your cards and put them in a pile, face down.

● Every word card has a missing mystery partner, which sounds the same but has a different meaning. To win a card, you must identify the meaning of both the card and its mystery partner.

● Read through the rules on the whiteboard.

● Agree which type of word each of you will collect, one partner wearing an 'S' label (same spelling homonyms), the other a 'D' (different spelling homophones).

● Take turns at turning over the top card. You can win it if it belongs to your group and you can prove its identity and think of its mystery partner. If not, the card goes to the bottom of the pile.

● When you have both claimed as many cards as you can, count up the ones you have won. Use a dictionary to find the mystery partners of the unclaimed cards.

NOW TRY THIS

Have you learned from each other? Find out by swapping over the 'S' and 'D' labels and playing the game again. Do you discover any new mystery partners?

WHICH WITCH?

OBJECTIVE: to examine the different spellings and meanings of common homophones
LEARNING LINK: auditory, visual
ORGANISATION: individual; small groups; whole class
RESOURCES: blank word cards and pens, for each child

Tip examples
Know always **k**icks off the answers.
Four c**ou**nts its letters.
Threw may be an arro**w**.
Grate has a **rat** warming itself.
Heard needs an **ear** to do its listening.

WHAT TO DO

● Write 'their' on a blank card, and 'there' on another.

● When the teacher says a sentence containing one of these words, hold up the correct word card (for example: *the witches have lost their broomsticks; there is panic at the meeting; their spells will not work!*).

● Continue the game with other common errors: 'no'/'know'; 'new'/'knew'; 'sea'/'see'; 'through'/'threw'; 'for'/'four'; 'great'/'grate', 'which'/'witch'; 'you'/'ewe'; 'herd'/'heard'.

● Which ones catch you out most often? Discuss these with the rest of the class and share a few memory tips (for example, 'new' is the opposite of 'old' so has the same number of letters; 'see' needs matching letters as a pair of glasses to look through) See box above for more examples.

● In small groups, devise memory tips to help others spell some of the words. It may be useful to make associations with other words or to link appearance with meaning.

● Share ideas as a class. Which ones do you find most memorable?

NOW TRY THIS

Make a memory tip display, finding a clever way to present it so that others will remember the visual image as well as the meaning.

TACTILE LEARNING

BINGO!

OBJECTIVE: to recognise and spell suffixes
LEARNING LINK: auditory, visual
ORGANISATION: individual; whole class
RESOURCES: a 3x3 grid of nine squares and colouring pencils or felt-tipped pens, for each child; a list of suffixes (see below) written on the whiteboard; a bag of word cards featuring root words (see below)

Suffixes
ship, hood, ness, ment, dom, like, ish, some, en, craft, ation, ate, ify, ise, less

Root words
child, nasty, manage, owner, champion, fair, silly, fit, neighbour, father, mother, govern, king, hand, wood, self, life, elastic, pure, pollen, apology, witch, length, dead, deep

WHAT TO DO

● You will be given a grid of nine squares. Write one of the suffixes from the whiteboard in each square.
● The teacher will call out root words. Try to put the root word called in front of one of your suffixes. If successful, tick the square containing that suffix and write the word you made on a piece of paper. Remember that the root word may need a small spelling change, such as changing its final 'y' to 'i', when it joins the suffix.
● The first player to make a row of small ticks (horizontal, vertical or diagonal) on their grid calls out *Bingo!* and wins a point.
● Continue to play until a player calls out *Full house!* to show that they have ticked every square. The teacher will check their words: if all are correct, that player receives the prize of five points. If there is a mistake, the game can restart.
● After a full house, start a new game with the same grid, but use a different coloured pen to tick the boxes.

NOW TRY THIS

Play again with a different set of root words.

SAMPLE ANSWERS
childhood, childish, childlike, childless; nastiness; management; ownership; championship; fairness, fairish; silliness; fitness; neighbourhood, neighbourless; fatherhood, fatherless; motherhood, motherless; government; kingdom, kingship, kinglike; handsome, handcraft, handless; woodlike, woodcraft, wooden, woodless; selfhood, selfness, selfish, selfless; life-like, lifeless; elasticate, elasticise, elastication; pureness, purify, purification; pollinate, pollenless, pollination; apologise; witchlike, witchcraft; lengthen; deaden; deepen

MISSING CHILDREN

OBJECTIVE: to spell words which differ in pronunciation but have common letter strings
LEARNING LINK: auditory, kinaesthetic, visual
ORGANISATION: groups of four
RESOURCES: a set of four 'sounds like' word cards (see below), for each group; a set of eight 'ough' word cards (see below), for each group; this activity can be used as a follow-up to 'Pronunciation practice'

'Sounds like' cards
cow, duff, sort, off

'ough' words
nought, trough, bough, tough, bought, cough, rough, plough

WHAT TO DO

● Get into groups of four. Each group member will receive a different 'sounds like' card.
● Each 'sounds like' parent must learn to recognise its own children! To claim them, you must be able to say their names correctly.
● Your group will be given a shuffled pack of eight cards, which will be placed face down in the centre of your group.
● One player turns over the top card. Everyone else in the group has 30 seconds to recognise and call out the name. If not, the word goes to the bottom of the pile, and the job of turning over the top card (and keeping silent and counting the seconds) passes to the next person.
● The winner is the 'sounds like' parent who first claims their two children. Afterwards, all eight words are collected, shuffled and a new pile is made for the game to restart.
● Which sound proves the most reliable parent?

NOW TRY THIS

Spread out the words face up and then claim them. Stand up, show your 'sounds like' card and prove you have the correct words by pronouncing them. Does the class agree that they sound like their children?

WHERE IN THE WORLD?

OBJECTIVE: to examine the properties of words ending in 'a', 'i', 'o' and 'u'
LEARNING LINK: visual
ORGANISATION: individual; pairs
RESOURCES: a word list (see below) written on the whiteboard; an etymological dictionary; a large sheet of paper and colouring pencils or felt-tipped pens, for each pair; this activity can be used as a follow-up to 'Trace our heritage'

Words

ravioli, piccolo, emu, panda, armadillo, concerto, risotto, chapatti, banjo, tagliatelli, tarantula, viola, oratorio, spaghetti, gecko

WHAT TO DO

● Look at the word list on the whiteboard and make sure you can read each word. Work with a partner to check you know their meanings.
● Use an etymological dictionary to find out each word's country of origin. (You may already have this information from *Trace our heritage*.)
● Choose one of the countries involved and act as their tourist officer. You need to design a new poster advertising your country and the words it has sent around the world.
● Think of an interesting way to show the country as well as the words to be included on the poster (for example, you could use national symbols and landmarks such as the Union Jack and Big Ben to represent England).

NOW TRY THIS

Take turns at presenting your poster to a group or the whole class. Is your poster approved for advertising space?

SPINNING JENNY

OBJECTIVE: to collect words with common roots
LEARNING LINK: visual
ORGANISATION: individual
RESOURCES: card, paper, scissors and pencils, for each child; a list of word roots (see below) written on the whiteboard

Word roots

dec (meaning 'ten'); cent (meaning 'hundred'); tele (meaning 'far'); port (meaning 'carry'); aqua (meaning 'water'); oct (meaning 'eight')

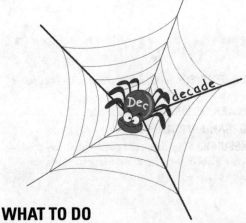

WHAT TO DO

● Jenny the spider needs help spinning her mini-webs. She already has the central pieces (word roots), but she needs at least three words with that root for each web.
● Draw six mini-webs on card, and cut them out. Write a root from the whiteboard in the centre of each web.
● For each web, plan and list on paper your three words. Jenny's web must not break, so check that the connecting words are correct!
● Add your words to the webs.

NOW TRY THIS

Stick your six mini-webs onto a poster in one large web.

JIGSAW FUN 1

OBJECTIVE: to recognise and create compound words
LEARNING LINK: kinaesthetic, visual
ORGANISATION: pairs
RESOURCES: firm card, scissors and felt-tipped pens, for each pair

WHAT TO DO

● Work with a partner. List ten compound words. Make sure that each compound word can be split into the two separate words it is made from (for example, 'lifeguard' separates into 'life' and 'guard').
● Work out a design for ten pairs of jigsaw pieces.
● Make your jigsaw pieces from firm card. For each pair of pieces, write one part of the compound word on one piece, the other part of the compound word on the other piece.
● Challenge another pair of children to do your jigsaw.

NOW TRY THIS

Shuffle your pieces, place them in a container, and swap with other pairs of children. Do you learn some new words?

JIGSAW FUN 2

OBJECTIVE: to recognise and create compound words

LEARNING LINK: kinaesthetic, visual

ORGANISATION: pairs

RESOURCES: jigsaw pieces from 'Jigsaw fun 1'; a large sheet of paper; glue and felt-tipped pens, for each pair

WHAT TO DO

● With a partner, stick your jigsaw pieces onto a large piece of paper to create a spelling poster. Leave a gap between the two jigsaw pieces (perhaps put an addition sign in the gap) to emphasise that two separate words create the one compound word.

● Add vivid illustrations to make the spellings more memorable.

NOW TRY THIS

Try out the spelling posters on one another. Do they help you remember the words and their spellings?

ARE YOU ABLE?

OBJECTIVE: to recognise and spell suffixes

LEARNING LINK: auditory, visual

ORGANISATION: individual; whole class

RESOURCES: a word list (see below) to be read out; two blank cards and a pen, for each child

Words

valuable, reliable, sensible, edible, enjoyable, probable, possible, breakable, disposable, miserable, terrible, irritable, incredible, invisible, curable, approachable, adorable, forgivable, indestructible, recognisable

WHAT TO DO

● Make two voting cards, one saying 'able', the other 'ible'.

● Listen as the teacher reads out a list of words ending in 'able' and 'ible'. After you hear each word, decide on the spelling of its ending and hold up the appropriate card.

● When the correct answer is written on the whiteboard, make a record of whether you got it right or wrong.

● Afterwards, investigate and discuss the completed list on the whiteboard. See if you can spot some spelling patterns and use them to put together general rules (see 'Answers').

NOW TRY THIS

Repeat the 'able' or 'ible' election. Are you now better at using your vote?

> **ANSWERS**
>
> Words ending in 'able' are more common. Dropping' able' generally leaves a recognisable word, for example 'enjoyable' beomes 'enjoy'; dropping 'ible' does not usually leave a complete word, for example 'invisible' becomes 'invis'. When a root word ends in 'e', you often drop the final 'e' and add 'able'.

CROCODILE SNAP!

OBJECTIVE: to distinguish between 'its' and 'it's'

LEARNING LINK: kinaesthetic, visual

ORGANISATION: pairs

RESOURCES: a 4x4 grid of 16 squares, card, a pen and scissors for each pair; the following words/ phrases written on the whiteboard: 'it is', 'it's', 'its', 'belonging to it'; this activity can be used as a follow-up to 'Space savers'

WHAT TO DO

● You and your partner will receive a page of 16 squares. Stick the sheet onto card.

● Look at the words on the whiteboard and write each word/phrase in a separate column four times. Then cut out 16 separate squares, making sure there are four squares for each word/phrase.

● You and your partner are going to play 'Crocodile snap!' One of you should shuffle the cards and deal eight to each of you.

● Hold all your cards so that no one else can see them.

● One player puts down a card in front of them, face up (for example, 'it is').

● If the other player, the crocodile, has a card with the same meaning ('it's'), they put it on top, say *Snap!* and win the pair (keeping them to one side). If they can't say *Snap!* in time (one minute), they must put down any card in front of them, waiting for that to be 'eaten' by the new crocodile.

● After eating, the crocodile puts down a card; otherwise players take turns putting down cards.

● At the end of a round, pick up your own unused cards and play again (pairs won are kept aside).

● After three rounds, the winner is the player with the most pairs.

NOW TRY THIS

Play the game again, reducing the time allowed for crocodiles to say 'Snap!'

TRAINED SPIES

OBJECTIVE: to investigate plural spelling patterns
LEARNING LINK: auditory, visual
ORGANISATION: individual; whole class
RESOURCES: lists of singular words ending in 'o' and their plurals (see below) written on the whiteboard; 'os' and 'oes' word cards, for each child; this activity can be used as a follow-up to 'Secret Agent J'

hero – heroes; banjo – banjos;
domino – dominoes; solo – solos; zoo – zoos;
volcano – volcanoes; flamingo – flamingoes;
disco – discos; igloo – igloos;
mango – mangoes; video – videos;
yoyo – yoyos; echo – echoes; piano – pianos;
casino – casinos; halo – haloes;
buffalo – buffaloes; patio – patios;
veto – vetoes; torpedo – torpedoes

WHAT TO DO

● Revise your training to become Secret Agent Jake – do you remember his LSCWC code? (He learns four spellings at a time, following the rules: Look at them; Say them; Cover them up; Write them; Check them.)
● Try out the code on four plurals from the list on the whiteboard. If you have not done the 'Secret Agent J' activity, use the code to learn all of the plural spellings on the list.
● If you are already trained, you will be given 'os' and 'oes' cards.
● The teacher will read out a singular 'o' word from the list (which should be covered up). When you hear the word, picture the spelling of its plural and hold up the correct card.
● After each word, the answer will be revealed so that you can keep count of your score.

NOW TRY THIS

Repeat the game with words ending in 'y'.

SPELL THOSE SUMS!

OBJECTIVE: to investigate pluralisation
LEARNING LINK: kinaesthetic, visual
ORGANISATION: individual; pairs
RESOURCES: list of words (see below) written on the whiteboard; a large sheet of paper, spare paper, a pencil and felt-tipped pens, for each child

Words
hero, fish, delay, photo, yacht, puppy, potato, trolley, lunch, dairy

WHAT TO DO

● Look at the list of singular words on the whiteboard.
● The plurals of these words often cause spelling problems. Numeracy may be the answer to these problems!
● Write and check the plural spellings of the words. On your own or with a partner, design and make a helpful plural poster, using combinations of the words; the symbols +, -, and =; and the letter 's'.

NOW TRY THIS

Present your poster to the rest of the class. Which sums produced surprising answers? (for example, 'puppy + s = puppies')

THE SKULKERS

OBJECTIVE: to identify spelling and pronunciation changes
LEARNING LINK: auditory, visual
ORGANISATION: individual; whole class
RESOURCES: list of words on display (see below); a large sheet of paper and felt-tipped pens, for each child

1. tie, fried, friend, receive
2. circle, cinema, simple, circus
3. keys, fees, trees, bees
4. pickle, kennel, kettle, wrinkle
5. eight, freight, height, weight
6. armour, pour, rumour, colour

WHAT TO DO

● Look at each set of words. Remind yourself of some general spelling rules linked to pronunciation.
● Remember that the spelling of a letter string may stay the same, but pronunciation may vary ('armour', 'rumour', 'pour').
● The spelling of a letter string may change, but it may still have the same sound ('pickle', 'kettle', 'kennel').
● We can call these rule-breakers 'Skulkers', as they skulk around and are easily missed!
● With the rest of the class, identify the Skulkers from the sets of words.
● Choose one that you think is likely to catch people out with its spelling or pronunciation. Create a poster to warn people about this word and to show the general rule that it breaks.

NOW TRY THIS

Present your poster to the rest of the class. Which ones will help them remember the Skulkers?

KINAESTHETIC LEARNING

ACTING TIME

OBJECTIVE: to recognise how the addition of 'ing' changes the spelling of verbs

LEARNING LINK: auditory, visual

ORGANISATION: individual; whole class

RESOURCES: ten verbs from the list (see below) written on a large whiteboard; the same verbs written on separate cards and placed in a box; a hall or a large area suitable for drama and movement

Verbs

do, chat, stare, enjoy, smile, meet, cut, take, tack, shape, shop, slide, ask, rid, tip, tape, hope, drive, look, jog, cry, shout, swim

WHAT TO DO

● It is 'Acting time'! Choose any of the words from the list on the whiteboard. You must not tell anyone the word you have chosen.

● While the teacher's eyes are closed, find a space in the classroom and start performing your action.

● The teacher will pull a verb card (for example, 'smile') from the box, and call *Freeze!*

● Freeze your action while the teacher reads out the card.

● If the teacher's card matches what you are doing, and you can spell it (for example, 'smiling'), award yourself one point for each (correct action and correct spelling).

NOW TRY THIS

Play the game again with ten different words from the list. Occasionally you will be challenged to spell your 'ing' verb. How many did you spell correctly? Can you think of any rules to help you when adding the 'ing' ending to a verb?

GOING FISHING

OBJECTIVE: to recognise how the addition of 'ing' changes the spelling of verbs

LEARNING LINK: auditory, tactile, visual

ORGANISATION: groups (large or small)

RESOURCES: a magnetic fishing rod (a stick with a piece of string and a magnet attached) for each child; fish-shaped word cards (see words below), each with a paper clip attached, a large plastic hoop, the spelling checklist (see below), group scoreboards and pens, for each group

Fish words

pull, tug, dive, hop, win, jump, hope, slip, scare, lose, fall, leap, race, surf

Spelling checklist

pulling, tugging, diving, hopping, winning, jumping, hoping, slipping, scaring, losing, falling, leaping, racing, surfing

WHAT TO DO

● You are going on a fishing trip! Form a group.

● The fish are swimming face down in the water, so it is difficult to identify them. You can catch them using magnetism, but, to keep them, you must correctly identify and change them.

● The fish-shaped words will be scattered face down in the ponds (large hoops).

● Take turns at fishing, using your fishing rod. When you catch a fish, you must turn it over, read the word that is written on it and write its 'ing' form and your own name on the group scoreboard.

● Use the checklist to check the spelling and, if your verb is correctly spelled, you can keep the fish; otherwise it must be thrown back into the pond.

● When all the fish have been caught, count your own catch. Who is today's star fisherman in your group?

NOW TRY THIS

Repeat the game, but this time, you have to explain the spelling rule in order to keep the fish.

CATCH IT!

OBJECTIVE: to practise the use of prefixes and suffixes
LEARNING LINK: auditory
ORGANISATION: whole class
RESOURCES: a ball or beanbag; list of word roots written on the whiteboard, as follows: 'super', 'prim', 'graph', 'phobia', 'trans', 'auto', 'micro', 'aero', 'ology'

WHAT TO DO

- Sit in a class circle.
- One person holds the ball or beanbag and says one of the roots on the whiteboard, such as *super*. When another person thinks of a word that uses this root (for example, *superman*), they should hold up their hand to have the ball. The ball is thrown to them. They say their word and wait for the next player to indicate that they have thought of another word with that root (for example, *supermarket*).
- Continue the game in this way. If there is a long pause (more than 90 seconds), start a new rally with a different word root. Which root produces the longest rally?

NOW TRY THIS

Play the game in smaller circles of eight to ten.

PLACES PLEASE!

OBJECTIVE: to investigate and learn to use the spelling pattern 'le'
LEARNING LINK: auditory, tactile, visual
ORGANISATION: groups of six
RESOURCES: individual letters written onto A4 paper to make six-lettered words (see below), with each set in a separate, numbered A4 envelope, for each group

Words
cackle, double, guzzle, dimple, rumble, candle, noodle, bottle, middle, feeble

WHAT TO DO

- Get into groups of six. Each group will receive an envelope of jumbled letters.
- Try to work out the word formed by these letters.
- Here is a clue to help you: 'To position your final two letters, just think of how my muddle has ended!'

- Remember to whisper your discussions as other groups will have to unscramble your envelope later. Let the teacher know when your group has finished. Holding up one letter each, can you arrange yourselves into the word ending in 'le'? Can you whisper the word?
- Return your letters to their envelope and take a new set.

NOW TRY THIS

Each group should tackle at least four envelopes. At the end, every group should be arranged as a word. Revise all of the words as a class.

HAPPY FAMILIES

OBJECTIVE: to investigate and learn to use the spelling pattern 'le'
LEARNING LINK: auditory, visual
ORGANISATION: individual; whole class
RESOURCES: a page of ten word beginnings (see below) and scissors for each child; large word-ending signs (see below) hung in different places around the classroom

Word beginnings
c, bun, chu, noo, pi, fa, cubi, reli, obsta, grum, pad, un, cir, can, prob, tri, rum, cy, t, hum, tri, swin, veget
Word endings for signs
able, dle, cle, ble, ckle, cle

WHAT TO DO

- Cut out the ten word beginnings from your page.
- The signs hung around the room are families. They show the endings for their family members.
- Choose one of your ten word beginnings, and go and 'join' a family.
- As you queue up to join your chosen family, the teacher will check your membership rights! You must be able to say your completed word and its correct spelling.
- Select another word beginning. Will you have to join a different family?

NOW TRY THIS

1. Play again, this time thinking of and writing your own word beginnings for your chosen family. Finish with everyone in a family.
2. Some family members (perhaps aided by a partner) will be asked to mime their words. Can the rest of the class work them out?

KINAESTHETIC LEARNING

SQUARE DANCE

OBJECTIVE: to create new words from existing knowledge of prefixes
LEARNING LINK: tactile, visual
ORGANISATION: groups of eight; pairs
RESOURCES: music; a blank word card and a pen, for each child; an elastic band for each group; scissors, for each pair

WHAT TO DO
● Take a blank card, and get into a group of eight.
● Choose a partner within your group. You and your partner will be allocated a prefix: 'dis', 'un', 'mis' or 'im'.
● Still working in pairs, write a word beginning with your allocated prefix on rough paper.
● Check it before you copy it onto card, with one partner writing the prefix and the other partner writing the rest of the word. Cut the word in half so that there are two cards – the prefix and the rest of the word.
● Put all of your group's eight cards together, shuffle them, put an elastic band around them and swap cards with another group.
● Get ready to take your partner for a square dance!
● When the music starts, a dealer in each group gives everyone a card. You must find your word partner within your group in order to form the group square before the music stops. Partners must stand next to each other to make the correct words and form one side of the square.
● Exchange shuffled card packs with another group and hold another dance.

NOW TRY THIS
This time, double up your groups, with 16 shuffled cards being shared among 16 dancers. Finish with a grand performance in which all the cards are shuffled and dealt to the whole class. How long will the music have to play before partners are matched in a class square?

> **POSSIBLE ANSWERS**
> dis: disagree, dishonest, disapprove, distrust, displease, disqualify, disobey, disallow
> un: unwell, unpopular, unkind, unpleasant, uncertain, unseen, unusual, unlucky
> mis: misunderstand, misplace, misprint, mislead, mis-spell, mistake, mistrust, misuse
> im: immature, impolite, imperfect, impossible, improbable, immigrate, immovable, improper

GET MULTIPLYING!

OBJECTIVE: to investigate spelling patterns in plurals
LEARNING LINK: tactile, visual
ORGANISATION: groups of four
RESOURCES: a page of five singular words (see below), two blank pieces of card, three pairs of scissors and four coloured PE bands, for each group

> **Sets of singular words**
> **1.** sister, hero, fox, fish, balloon
> **2.** meal, church, word, lunch, girl
> **3.** chimney, watch, hiss, house, bus
> **4.** patch, dish, school, cargo, box
> **5.** dog, patch, monkey, wish, latch
> **6.** brush, boy, ditch, disc, hoax

WHAT TO DO
● Get into groups of four. Your group will be given a page of five words and matching, coloured PE bands.
● One group member should cut out the words, while one makes a letter 'e' from card, another makes a letter 's' and another prepares a page for recording answers.
● The group member who has the words is singular and wants to be multiplied! When they hold up a word, 'e' and 's' must decide whether one or both of them need to stand beside the singular group member.
● After offering advice, the recorder writes down the agreed plural.
● Once finished, put on your bands to signal that you are ready for a score check by the teacher. (Your group wins a point for each correct plural.)
● Then start again, changing roles and using a new set of words.

NOW TRY THIS
Discuss the correct plurals with the rest of your group. Is there a pattern? Are there any rules for which words like 'e' and 's'? Test your theories on some new word cards of your own. Share your results as a class.

SSSH!

OBJECTIVE: to read and spell words containing silent letters
LEARNING LINK: auditory, visual
ORGANISATION: groups of five
RESOURCES: a small whiteboard and a marker pen, for each child; word list (see below)

Words

5 letters: crumb, wring, gnash, knife, kneel, write, sword, rhyme, wrist, whine, doubt, would, knock, plumb, thumb, gnome, whale, rhino, chalk, could, whirl, wheat

4 letters: yolk, numb, gnat, lamb, knot, when, half, know, knit, calm, calf, folk, knob, tomb, debt

WHAT TO DO

● Stand side by side in a team of five.
● A five-letter word will be assigned to your team and one of its letters will be assigned to each team member. Use your individual whiteboard to write the letter.
● You have to work out which of them is a silent letter. Say the word aloud, listening for a letter that does not make itself heard.
● You have two minutes to decide. Then, if you think you have the silent letter, put your finger against your lips. The teacher will tell you whether you are correct.
● Play again with new words. Sometimes you will be given a four-letter word, so that one team member can concentrate on listening while the rest say the word.
● As your team improves, the teacher will reduce the amount of thinking time allowed!

NOW TRY THIS

In a harder version of the game, the letters will be assigned in a jumbled order.

SCRAMBLED EGGS

OBJECTIVE: to improve spelling by using anagrams
LEARNING LINK: tactile, visual
ORGANISATION: groups of four
RESOURCES: word cards (see below); a small whiteboard and a marker pen, for each child; a timer

Word cards

race, coma, lady, safe, keys, with, then, love, vein, heir, diet, veil, pier

WHAT TO DO

● Get into groups of four. Your group will receive a four-letter word card to keep secret.
● Use your individual whiteboards to make the word, with each member of the group writing one of the four letters on their whiteboard. 'Scramble' the word in the best way to disguise it. How should you order yourselves?
● Each group shows itself to the class. If someone works out the identity of the word, they win two points.
● After 90 seconds, if no one guesses the word correctly, the group unscrambles itself and each group member wins a point.

NOW TRY THIS

1. Repeat the game, but this time, only 60 seconds are allowed for thinking. Does anyone ever spot an alternative identity for the same letters (for example, 'care' and 'race')?
2. Play with bigger groups and longer words.

GREEDY PARTNERS

OBJECTIVE: to create compound words
LEARNING LINK: auditory, tactile, visual
ORGANISATION: whole class
RESOURCES: four washing lines (one in each corner of the classroom); pegs; 12 base-word cards (see below), three pegged on to each of the washing lines; paper clips, a pen and small labels, for each child

Base words

day, no, any, some, time, every, eye, sand, out, play, one, body, green, in, thing, head, where, woman, hand, man, mouth, sun

WHAT TO DO

● Write a small name label for yourself, and gather in the central area of the classroom with the rest of your class.
● Look at the base words on the washing lines.
● You can choose any base word to attach your name to (with a paper clip). However, you must be able to add a front or back to your chosen word, to create a compound word, for example, 'everyone'.
● When you have made your decision, attach your name and move to that corner.
● You will be asked to say the compound you have made. Which greedy base word got the most partners?

NOW TRY THIS

Try again with a different set of base words.

DAISY CHAIN

OBJECTIVE: to recognise and create compound words

LEARNING LINK: auditory

ORGANISATION: whole class

RESOURCES: the list of base words from 'Greedy partners' written on the whiteboard

WHAT TO DO

● Stand in a circle with the rest of your class. Look at the list of base words on the whiteboard. You are going to find out which ones make the longest chains.

● The first person will start the chain by saying a common base word (for example, *play*). The next person must add a completion word that forms a compound (for example, *ground*) and take their hand in order to start the chain. Move together to the third person, who must say a different completion word (for example, *mate*), and link them to your chain.

● Remember, the aim is to make chains of two or more compounds. A chain must begin with one of the base words. If a player gets stuck, they must start a new chain by saying an unused base word. Once a chain is finished, its members return to the circle.

● Start the first chain. The teacher will tick off the base words as they are used, keep count of the number of compounds each base word produces, and make a separate 'failure' list of the words that do not manage to make a long enough chain. Which base word wins?

NOW TRY THIS

Change your place in the circle. Now try again with the words on the 'failure' list. Does the circle make better daisy chains this time?

IF THE HAT FITS…

OBJECTIVE: to use the apostrophe to spell contracted forms of words

LEARNING LINK: auditory, visual

ORGANISATION: groups of six

RESOURCES: a list of full forms (no longer than five letters; see below) to be read out; a small whiteboard and a marker pen for each child; a hat with apostrophe written or stuck on it, for each group

---

Full forms

he is; I am; he has; it has; do not; is not; I had; I have; I will; she is; it is; he will

---

WHAT TO DO

● Get into a group of six, and choose one group member to wear the apostrophe hat.

● The teacher will read out the full form of a phrase (for example, *I am*).

● Make the words of the phrase, with each group member (except the apostrophe) writing a letter on their individual whiteboard. Stand in order, with your boards in front of you.

● Now make the contraction of the phrase ('I'm'). Decide which group members will be removed and replaced by the apostrophe.

● The teacher will move around the room and let you know if the contraction is right.

NOW TRY THIS

Each group presents a two-act play to the class, featuring the full form and the contraction. Were the correct actors replaced for the second act?

EXTRAS

OBJECTIVE: to improve spelling of commonly mis-spelled words

LEARNING LINK: auditory, visual

ORGANISATION: groups of four

RESOURCES: word cards with the problematic letter highlighted (see below), one for each group

---

Word cards

su**r**prise, hop**p**ing, **k**night, cu**p**board, mini**a**ture, jewell**e**ry, lot**t**ery, han**d**kerchief, gover**n**ment, r**h**ythm, Feb**r**uary, ras**p**berry, enviro**n**ment, ge**o**graphy, We**d**nesday

---

WHAT TO DO

● The classroom is a film set. Film extras usually have minor roles with no lines to speak, but today the extras will star! They will be the only ones to speak.

● Your group will receive a word card. The highlighted letter is often forgotten: the extra.

● Work out a short scene to convey your word's meaning and make up some lines for the extra to speak. For example: for 'surprise', the scene could involve friends busily doing things when a newcomer (the extra) suddenly appears and makes them jump. The newcomer introduces himself and says a clue to help watchers guess the word: *I'm the rascal 'r' who gives a shock to really remember!*

NOW TRY THIS

Perform your film for the rest of the class. Can the audience guess the word?

MIX AND MATCH

OBJECTIVE: to recognise and create compound words
LEARNING LINK: visual
ORGANISATION: whole class
RESOURCES: compound words divided into two separate words and written on cards (one card for each child; see below)

Compound words

Set 1: churchyard, sideboard, dustbin, playground, goalkeeper, somewhere, anything, clockwise, earthworm, gunpowder, breakfast, weekend, nowhere, upstairs, downstairs, nothing, deadline

Set 2: windmill, bricklayer, anyone, someone, cupboard, lifeguard, classroom, football, paintbrush, everywhere, anywhere, handbag, eyebrow, housekeeper, greenhouse, sunrise, daylight

---

CHARADES

OBJECTIVE: to identify words within words
LEARNING LINK: auditory, visual
ORGANISATION: groups of four; whole class
RESOURCES: a list of long words from 'Detective work' and additional words (see below) written on the whiteboard

---

Additional words
workmanship, knighthood, childhood, photocopy, antennae

WHAT TO DO

● In a group of four, secretly select a word from the list on the whiteboard.
● You are going to play 'Word charades'. Each group must mime their word for the rest of the class to guess. The trick is to break down the word and mime the parts in order, so that the audience can build the word in their mind. (You may have to leave out bits of the word.)
● Here are some useful miming tips: touch your ear to indicate that 'this only sounds like the word it represents' ('shall' instead of the mimed 'pal'); use your hands in a stretching or shrinking movement to indicate that an oral guess needs stretching ('can' into 'cans') or reducing ('ink' into 'in').
● If the audience calls out part of your word correctly while you are miming, you should make a thumbs-up sign before moving on to the next part.
● Which words take the longest time to guess? Do some words prove impossible?

NOW TRY THIS

If any words have not yet been mimed successfully, collaborate as a class to produce a mime that will work.

WHAT TO DO

● Today the classroom is divided into three areas: Front, Back and Compound.
● Your class will be split into two: half in the Front area, half in the Back.
● You will be given an appropriate card, featuring the front or back of a compound word (from Set 1). You can win admittance to the prized Compound area by linking with someone in the other half of the class.
● When the game starts, mingle with the others and search for a compatible partner. When sure of your selection, both of you move to the Compound area.
● The Compound area is well-guarded by your teacher, and only partners who are well-matched and know their compound word will be admitted!
● Play the game again with different words (Set 2).

NOW TRY THIS

At the end of the game, turn yourself into a new compound word by changing your front or back. Write your new word on card and display it in the class.

KINAESTHETIC LEARNING

WORD PERFECT!

OBJECTIVE: to create new words using existing knowledge of prefixes
LEARNING LINK: auditory, tactile, visual
ORGANISATION: individual
RESOURCES: a list of 14 prefixes (see below) written on the whiteboard; 14 hats with the prefixes written or stuck on them

Prefixes
re, de, anti, bi, contra, ab, in, pre, non, inter, ex, un, sub, mis

WHAT TO DO

● You are auditioning for a part in a new play, called *Word Perfect*.
● The 14 prefixes on the whiteboard are the parts that are available.
● Select a part to audition for. You will need to be able to say three words starting with that prefix.
● Take turns at putting on your chosen prefix hat and saying your words. The teacher will keep a record of interesting word choices.

NOW TRY THIS

In the second round of auditions, everyone has to try for a new part. You will do particularly well if you can think of some 'new lines' (different words).

COMEDY HOUR

OBJECTIVE: to explore homonyms with the same spelling but multiple meanings
LEARNING LINK: auditory
ORGANISATION: pairs; whole class
RESOURCES: a list of homonyms from 'Alphabet muddle' written on the whiteboard; some paper and a pencil, for each child

WHAT TO DO

● It is time for some comedy!
● Working with a partner, make up a joke or funny story involving confusion over the multiple meanings of a homonym. For example:
'You're a tall lad,' said Mr Yorke to Jason, the new zoo trainee. 'It's a hot day, so cool that crane down for me.' It was difficult reaching the top of the crane, but Jason managed. 'You stupid boy!' bawled Mr Yorke, when he returned later. 'You're supposed to look after animals here, not dress the builder's machine in a sunhat!'

● Choose a homonym from the list on the whiteboard and make notes with your partner for your story or joke. Practise telling it, and decide who will say what. Remember, a comedian needs good timing.
● Stroll around the classroom as travelling entertainers, telling one another your jokes.

NOW TRY THIS

In groups, discuss the joke you found most memorable. Write the homonym involved on your individual whiteboard. After a show of boards, which homonym wins the funny vote?

FREEZE-FRAMES

OBJECTIVE: to examine the different spellings and meanings of common homophones
LEARNING LINK: visual
ORGANISATION: groups of six; pairs
RESOURCES: separate lists of six jumbled homophones (see below) for each group

Homophones
no, know; new, knew; sea, see; through, threw; for, four; great, grate; you, ewe; which, witch; herd, heard; be, bee; hole, whole; morning, mourning; place, plaice; right, write; might, mite; through, threw; I, eye

WHAT TO DO

● Get into groups of six. Your group will be given a muddled list of six words that make three pairs of homonyms.
● Allocate one word to each member of your group. Can you work out who is your homophone partner?
● Now work with your homophone partner to devise poses that will show your meanings.
● When you have decided, assume your pose and freeze in position.
● The teacher will move among the groups, carrying out random checks on pronunciation and understanding, asking each frozen word: *Who are you? What do you mean?*

NOW TRY THIS

As a group, take turns at presenting your freeze-frames to the rest of the class. When the teacher holds up your group's list of words, can the audience recognise which pair of homophones is which?

ROOT AND BRANCH

OBJECTIVE: to recognise and spell suffixes
LEARNING LINK: tactile, visual
ORGANISATION: whole class
RESOURCES: suffix cards (one for each child; see below); one set of root word cards (see below); this activity can be used as a follow-up to 'Bingo!'

Suffixes

al, ary, ic, ship, hood, ious, ness, dom, like, ly, ish, some, en, craft, ate, ling

Root words

infect, person, atom, mission, angel, child, mother, length, witch, king, brother, fair, elastic, hand, deep, sap, member

---

WHAT TO DO

● As a class, form a large circle.
● Each pair of you will receive a suffix card. You are branches looking for a tree to grow on. Perhaps you will be lucky today!
● The teacher stands in the middle of the circle, representing a tree – an ever-changing one.
● The teacher declares and shows the name of the tree (a root word). Work out if your suffix can be attached to the tree to form a word. If it can, go and stand by the tree.
● Successful branches should sit together to one side of the tree. Then the tree's identity (root word) changes. Can any unattached branches grow on it now?
● At the end of the game, see which branches were lucky and found somewhere to grow. Which type of tree did they grow on?

NOW TRY THIS

Play the game again, with a different suffix card.

ANSWERS
infect: infectious
person: personal, personhood
atom: atomic
mission: missionary
angel: angelic, angelical
child: childhood, childlike, childish
mother: motherhood, motherlike, motherly, mothercraft
length: lengthy, lengthen
witch: witchlike, witchcraft
king: kingship, kinghood, kingdom, kinglike, kingly
brother: brotherly, brotherhood
fair: fairness, fairish, fairly
elastic: elasticate
hand: handsome, handling
deep: deeply, deepen
sap: sapling
member: membership

LIVING WORDS

OBJECTIVE: to spell the endings of regular verbs
LEARNING LINK: auditory, visual
ORGANISATION: groups of seven
RESOURCES: verb lists (see below); a small whiteboard and a marker pen, for each child

---

Verbs

List 1 (for groups of 7 children): try, save, fix, cry, play, wish, spy, hug, show, buzz, note, save, frame

List 2 (for groups of 8 children): drop, carry, drag, grab, hurry, shop, shun, trim

---

WHAT TO DO

● Get into groups of seven. Your group will be instructed to make one of the words from List 1 (for example, *Make a three-letter verb ending in 'y'*).
● Arrange yourselves in the correct order, with your letters written on your individual whiteboards in front of you.
● Then you will receive a further instruction to follow (for example, *Add 's' to your verb; Make it past with 'ed'; Add 'ing'*).
● Remember that some letters may need to be removed as well as added!
● The teacher will move around among the groups, constantly checking spellings as letters are added or altered.
● The game continues, using a new starting verb.

NOW TRY THIS

1. One group will be asked to select a verb from List 2 and add 'ing'. (Do they realise they need the teacher as an additional letter?)
2. In groups of eight, play the game again with List 2 verbs.

PLAYING SOFTBALL

OBJECTIVE: to investigate the effect of adding suffixes to words ending in 'f' and 'fe'
LEARNING LINK: auditory
ORGANISATION: whole class
RESOURCES: four hard balls of a matching colour; four soft balls of a different matching colour

WHAT TO DO

- You are going to play a ball game. The hard, red balls represent 'fs', and the soft, blue ones represent 'ves'. (The letters could be written on the balls.)
- Make a circle around the teacher who will call out a child's name and throw or roll a ball to them.
- If your name is called, say a plural word that ends with the letters on the ball. Remember to consider how the word is pronounced and whether it has a hard or soft sound.
- If you are correct, you become the central player, in charge of the balls.
- As the game continues, try to use new words.

NOW TRY THIS

Play the game in groups, each with its own set of red and blue balls.

WIND THE CLOCK

OBJECTIVE: to recognise and spell suffixes
LEARNING LINK: auditory, visual
ORGANISATION: individual; whole class
RESOURCES: a list of suffixes (see below) written on the whiteboard; a small whiteboard and a marker pen, for each child

Suffixes
hood, ship, ness, ment, al, ary, ic, ive, ible, able, tion, sion, ation, ution, cian

WHAT TO DO

- Choose a suffix from the list and write it on your individual whiteboard to hold in front of you.
- Together create a human suffix clock: hold your suffix and form a large class circle, while the teacher stands in the centre as the arrow.
- With their eyes shut, the teacher will spin round and stop, pointing to one person in the circle.
- If the teacher ends up pointing to you, you must say a word ending with your suffix. Otherwise you are out!

- Play a second round of the game, in which words cannot be used more than once.

NOW TRY THIS

Play again with new suffixes or with a short time limit for answers.

CATCH THE POST!

OBJECTIVE: to spell words with common endings
LEARNING LINK: tactile, visual
ORGANISATION: whole class
RESOURCES: word beginnings on separate cards (a selection for each child; see below); five common ending labels to be worn by human postboxes (see below)

Word beginnings
sl, glor, infect, reac, alth, soc, br, promo, obv, thr, ser, n, offic, ambit, en, part, subtrac, c, r, electrocu, finance

Ending labels
ious, tion, ial, ough, ight

WHAT TO DO

- Your classroom is a town. The teacher and the teaching assistant are the postboxes for the whole town. You will be given some word beginnings to post.
- The postboxes only accept the letters that fit their special ending label; the label changes with the postbox's location.
- The postboxes take up positions on different sides of the 'street', and wait to receive the post. You must work out if your word beginnings plus either postbox's ending will make a word. If it does, hand in your post.
- After two minutes, the collection closes. The postboxes change their labels and move to a new spot in town.
- How many times do the postboxes have to change before the class has posted everything?

NOW TRY THIS

The word beginnings are shuffled and handed out again, but on this occasion you have less time to catch the post!

ANSWERS
slight, glorious, infectious, reaction, although, social, bright, promotion, obvious, through, serious or serial, night, officious or official, ambitious, enough, partial, subtraction, cough, right or rough, electrocution, financial

SPIDERS, SPIDERS, EVERYWHERE!

OBJECTIVE: to identify groups of words with common roots
LEARNING LINK: auditory, visual
ORGANISATION: whole class
RESOURCES: common roots (see below) written on sticky labels; six child-sized cardboard sandwich-boards with one root word label on each; this activity can be used as a follow-up to 'Spinning Jenny'

Roots
micro (meaning 'small'); fort (meaning 'strong'); scope (meaning 'see'); ped (meaning 'foot'); dent (meaning 'tooth'); multi (meaning 'many'); dec (meaning 'ten'); cent (meaning 'hundred'); tele (meaning 'far'); port (meaning 'carry'); aqua (meaning 'water'); oct (meaning 'eight')

WHAT TO DO

● Six children are appointed as spiders, and are given root bodies (sandwich-boards) to wear. They need words to make their webs.
● They must move around, encouraging the rest of the class (who need to be able to think of a suitable word) to join them.
● As a class, look together at the finished webs. Which spider's web is largest?

NOW TRY THIS

Play again with different root words.

MAKE YOURSELF HEARD

OBJECTIVE: to aid the spelling of compound words
LEARNING LINK: auditory, visual
ORGANISATION: whole class; groups of seven or eight
RESOURCES: compound words (see below) written on the whiteboard; a small whiteboard and a marker pen for each child; this activity can be used as a follow-up to 'Hear what you see'

Compound words
headline, football, postcard, goodbye, windfall, deadline, footnote, bonfire, outdoor

---

WHAT TO DO

● As a class, discuss the meaning of the words on the whiteboard. Can you spot what they have in common? (They are all compounds.)

● One child will be chosen to say the words aloud. Can the rest of the class identify one letter in each that is not pronounced clearly?
● Nine children will be chosen to stand at the front. Each will be given a letter from the word 'frostbite', to write on their whiteboard and hold up so that they form the word. Can you identify the letter that might cause a spelling problem? (the first 't')
● Here is a way to remember this letter: 't' is lurking in 'frostbite' to nip your *toes!*'
● Now get into groups of seven or eight. A word will be assigned to each group.
● Work out and experiment with a mnemonic or memory trick to help spellers remember the problem letter in your word.
● Present your results to the rest of the class.

NOW TRY THIS

Repeat the activity with new words.

HERE COME THE ROBOTS!

OBJECTIVE: to spell polysyllabic words containing unstressed vowels
LEARNING LINK: auditory, visual
ORGANISATION: individual; whole class
RESOURCES: word cards (see below)

Word cards
hospital, lottery, prepare, definite, general, library, interest, family, easily, primary, separate, familiar, factory, miserable, difference, carpet, business, doctor, reference

---

WHAT TO DO

● Listen as the teacher says the word 'separate' in a casual way, and look at it written down on a card. Which unstressed vowel was difficult to hear? (the first 'a')
● Perhaps spelling would be easier if everyone talked like robots! Listen as the teacher says the word again, breaking it into distinct syllables ('se-par-ate'), with vowels carefully pronounced.
● The teacher will display four word cards and cast a spell to turn your class into walking robots.
● When you hear the words *Time to robot chat*, have a conversation with the nearest robot, making sure you use the four words displayed.
● After one minute, a new set of words will be displayed. Read them and then continue on your way until the next call of *Time to robot chat*.

NOW TRY THIS

Learn other tricky spellings using robot talk!

TICKETS, PLEASE

OBJECTIVE: to recognise and use common suffixes
LEARNING LINK: visual
ORGANISATION: whole class
RESOURCES: suffixes (see below) written on individual cards; this activity can be used as a follow-up to 'Race for pay'

Suffixes
ible, able, ive, tion, sion, cian, ssion, ation, ful, ution

WHAT TO DO
● Your classroom is the foyer of a multi-screen cinema.
● Admittance to each of the films being shown is strictly by ticket only. There are only seven seats available for each film.
● Five people will be chosen to hold up the suffix film titles.
● Think of a word ending in one of the suffixes and write it on paper. If your ticket is correct, you will be allowed in to watch your chosen film. Which film closes for admission first?
● Start again, but this time you have to watch a different film.

NOW TRY THIS
Play again with new suffix film titles.

FRIENDS UNITED

OBJECTIVE: to distinguish between 'its' and 'it's'
LEARNING LINK: visual
ORGANISATION: individual; whole class
RESOURCES: four words/phrases written on the whiteboard: 'it is', 'it's', 'its', 'belonging to it'; a small whiteboard and a marker pen for each child; this activity can be used as a follow-up to 'Crocodile snap!'

WHAT TO DO
● Copy one of the words/phrases on the whiteboard on to your individual whiteboard.
● Travel back in time to Reception class! Everyone is anxious to find a friend. The word/phrase you have written is now your name. You can only be friends with someone who has the same name written in a different way.
● Mingle with the rest of the class, holding your identification whiteboard in front of you as you search for a friend (someone with a board that means the same as yours but is expressed differently).

● Sit down when you find a friend. Who will be lucky?
● Play again, this time writing a new identity on your whiteboard.

NOW TRY THIS
Clear your own whiteboard while the teacher clears theirs. You will be put in pairs at random and asked to write matching identities on your whiteboards. When finished, the whole class holds up their whiteboards. Are friends united?

ROLL THE DICE

OBJECTIVE: to identify plural spelling patterns
LEARNING LINK: auditory, tactile, visual
ORGANISATION: pairs
RESOURCES: a paper or card playing board of 16 squares (as in 'Crocodile snap!') and a list of plurals (see below) for each pair; a large cardboard dice with a spelling rule written on each side (see below)

Plurals
potatoes, worries, foxes, babies, keys, hisses, lollies, plays, trousers, tries, chimneys, diaries, sheep, turkeys, holidays, heroes, deer, banjos, scissors, dominoes, solos, zoos, news, watches, flamingoes, discos, mangoes, yoyos, echoes, churches

Plural spelling rules to be written on dice
has no singular
change a singular 'y' to 'ies'
+ es
+ s to a singular 'y'
+ es to a singular 'o'
same in singular and plural

WHAT TO DO
● Find a partner. When you receive your playing board and list of plurals, write a plural word in each square on the board.
● The teacher acts as caller, rolling the dice and calling out the rule on the uppermost face. You and your partner have 30 seconds to tick all the words following that rule on your board. The teacher will check that you are correct.
● A point is awarded to the first pair with a complete line of ticks (horizontal or vertical).
● Resume the game after each line call. Does anyone manage a full card?

NOW TRY THIS
Start a new game. This time, cross out the ticks to match the calls. Compare scores.

FAMISHED FOXES

OBJECTIVE: to identify plural spelling patterns
LEARNING LINK: tactile, visual
ORGANISATION: groups of four; whole class
RESOURCES: lists of singular nouns (see below); a small whiteboard and a marker pen, for each child

---

Sets of four singular nouns
drink, dish, diet, dial
plank, prow, paint, patch
tortoise, tomato, trousers, twirl
bridge, box, boy, brook
clasp, church, crisp, curl
school, sock, six, scene
turnip, tray, tax, twist
wish, way, wisp, whistle
lump, lunch, lock, lettuce
radio, radish, ray, rose
bean, balloon, bunch, bridle
house, hutch, hint, husk
bus, ball, banana, bee
deer, dormouse, duck, domino
volcano, vixen, van, vat

WHAT TO DO

● Famished foxes are on the prowl for food. They can only eat food they can add 'es' to.
● Four children are chosen to be foxes. They must cover their eyes or wait where they cannot see what is going on.
● The rest of the class forms groups of four, each group with a list of four singular words.
● Allocate a word to each member of your group and then write them on individual whiteboards. One of these is possible food for a fox (it takes 'es' for its plural).
● Position yourselves around the room, holding your whiteboards in front of you. Think about where in your group the 'es' person should stand to have the best hope of fooling the foxes.
● The foxes are set loose! Can they find all their 'es' prey in the three-minute feeding time?

NOW TRY THIS

Play again in new groups with new foxes.

ELECTRICITY WIRES

OBJECTIVE: to use word roots and derivations
LEARNING LINK: auditory
ORGANISATION: whole class
RESOURCES: word roots (see below) written on the whiteboard

Word roots
act, light, child, take, electric, hand, joy, machine, bore, obey, relate, pack, govern, prove

---

WHAT TO DO

● The class is arranged in two lines of pylons, A and B, facing each other.
● Words should bounce back and forth between them so their lines are joined up with a criss-cross network of electrical word wires.
● If there is a break (a silence longer than 30 seconds), the electrical power fails and that line of pylons forfeits a point.
● The teacher stands at the start of line A and switches on the flow of electricity by saying a word root (for example, *act*). The next player (the first person in line B) has to say an associated word (perhaps *action*), and then the next person in line A has to say a second associated word (such as *actor*).
● This word chain can continue (for example, with *activity* and *actual*) or, after two association words, the next player is free to start again with a new word root. If a player does manage a third associated word, they win a bonus point for their line of pylons.
● Play the game using the list of root words on the whiteboard. Does the electricity keep flowing? Which pylons are strongest?

NOW TRY THIS

You can gain even more experience of extending your vocabulary by forming shorter lines for group games.

KINAESTHETIC LEARNING

ANSWERS
tion: direction, action
cian: electrician, magician, optician
sion: extension, explosion, persuasion
ssion: discussion, oppression, possession
ation: education, translation, foundation
etion: completion, deletion
ition: competition, repetition, opposition
otion: devotion, promotion
ution: contribution, pollution, contribution

MUSICAL HATS!

OBJECTIVE: to recognise and spell suffixes
LEARNING LINK: auditory, tactile, visual
ORGANISATION: whole class
RESOURCES: nine hats featuring the suffixes 'tion', 'cian', 'sion', 'ssion', 'ation', 'etion', 'ition', 'otion' and 'ution'; word cards (see below); music

Word cards
electric, contribute, extend, pollute, discuss, complete, educate, contribute, optic, devote, compete, direct, magic, possess, delete, persuade, act, translate, promote, repeat, oppress, explode, oppose, found

HUMAN LETTERS

OBJECTIVE: to investigate and establish rules for consonant spelling patterns
LEARNING LINK: auditory, tactile, visual
ORGANISATION: whole class
RESOURCES: sticky labels with 'ca', 'ce', 'ci', 'co' or 'cu' written on them; a small whiteboard and a marker pen, for each child

WHAT TO DO

● You need plenty of space for this activity. Gather in the main, central area of the classroom.
● Nine children will be given suffix hats to wear. They must stand outside the central area.
● Everyone else will receive a word card. When the music plays, you have one to two minutes to join a suffix to create a new word. (They will probably require spelling changes.)
● When the music stops, anyone who is not at a 'hat' stand must return to the centre. The teacher checks the words that are in place. If one is wrong, it is sent back to the centre.
● Then the music restarts, so that anyone without a place can search again.
● After three rounds, a point is awarded to all the words correctly placed and to suffixes with all their words. Take turns to call out your new words. What do they have in common? (They all sound like 'shun'.) You can win an additional point if you know the spelling changes that are needed.

WHAT TO DO

● Five children in your class are postboxes, with a different label on each one.
● The rest of the class are letters, responsible for addressing and posting themselves.
● Write your address word, including 'c + vowel' (for example, 'cabbage' or 'lace') on your individual whiteboard and go to the appropriate postbox. Each box can hold only seven letters, and so if it is full, you must write a different 'c + vowel' word and try another box.
● The teacher will check that everyone is at the appropriate postbox.

NOW TRY THIS

1. Take turns to call out your address. What do the listeners notice?
2. Now go to the sorting office, where all the hard sounds go to one side, and soft sounds to the other. Which postboxes take their mail to the same side?

CHAMELEONS

OBJECTIVE: to recognise and use common suffixes
LEARNING LINK: tactile, visual
ORGANISATION: groups of five
RESOURCES: pairs of words (see below) written on separate word cards, one pair for each group; a small whiteboard and a marker pen, for each child

---

Pairs of words
hood – loom; bough – cough; dear – heard; pour – flour; pie – tried; fried – lied; right – weight

---

WHAT TO DO

● Get into groups of five. Two members of your group will receive a word card.
● Those two members are chameleons, one changing into the other when needed. However, they always keep their body (the main letter string, for example *'oo'*; *'ough'*; *'ear'*; *'our'*; *'ie'*; *'ight'*).
● The chameleons can only change gradually: with one letter at a time being added, removed or changed to form a real word.
● With your whole group, work out how to manage the change. How many steps can you manage it in? What words will the chameleons become?
● Write the intervening words on individual whiteboards and arrange yourselves in order with the two chameleons on the ends of the row.

NOW TRY THIS

Pairs of chameleons present their changes to the class. Which has the quickest change (the fewest steps)? Play again with other word pairs.

STAND-UP COMEDY

OBJECTIVE: to explore the differences between homophones
LEARNING LINK: auditory
ORGANISATION: pairs or groups of three
RESOURCES: homophone riddles from 'Riddle me' (this activity can be used as a follow-up)

WHAT TO DO

● Look at your riddles from 'Riddle me'.
● You are going to take part in a Victorian concert, where a series of performers stand up and ask quick riddles.

● Rehearse your performance with a partner or in a group of three. 'Plant' someone in the audience to jump up and spell out the answer.
● Start your concert!

NOW TRY THIS

Can you write more riddles, this time leaving the audience to work out the answer?

MUSICAL MATS

OBJECTIVE: to recognise the spelling and meaning of prefixes
LEARNING LINK: auditory, visual
ORGANISATION: whole class
RESOURCES: word cards (see below); five labels featuring the prefixes 'in', 'un', 'ir', 'il' and 'im'; hall or similar large space; five PE mats laid out on the floor; music (this activity could be done with half the class at a time)

Word cards
mature, legible, responsible, patient, accurate, likely, regular, convenient, possible, literate, resistible, well, known, capable, legal, rational, polite, certain, attentive

---

WHAT TO DO

● Five children will be asked to wear a prefix label and stand next to one of the PE mats.
● Everyone else spreads out, leaving the mats out of bounds. When the music starts, skip around, keeping off the mats.
● The teacher and teaching assistant mingle with the class, giving each child a word card.
● When the music stops, you must read your word, spot the prefix that will turn you into your opposite, and sit on that mat.
● If you manage to sit on a mat, you must hand your word card over to the teacher for checking. You can only stay if you can say your new word and are sitting on the correct mat.
● The music will be played again to allow time for the unplaced children to find a mat.

NOW TRY THIS

Play the complete game again, but you will have less time to find a mat. If you run out of time, you are out of the game.

Name _____   Date _____

Bubble trouble

Write the correct word under each clue.

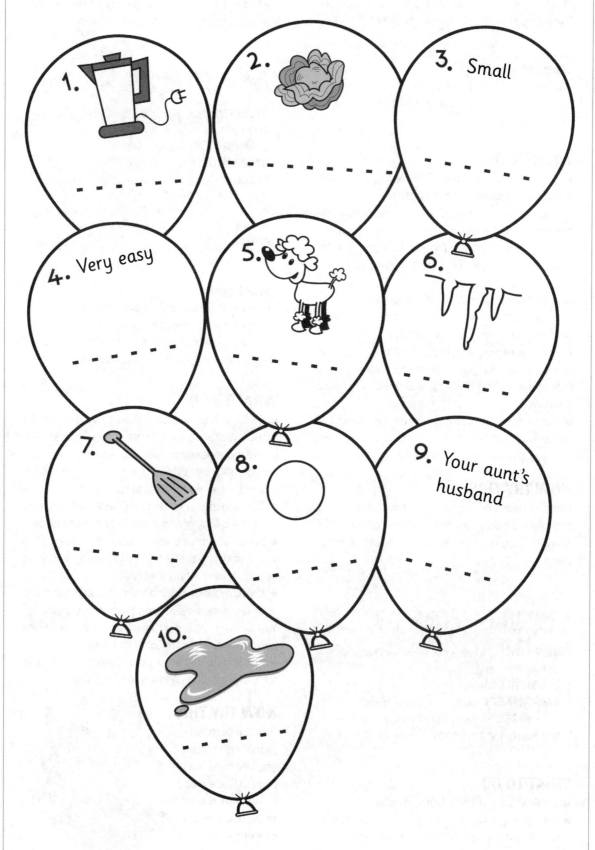

DAILY SPELLING TEASERS FOR AGES 7–11

Polygon puzzle 1 and 2

■ Rearrange some of the letters in each polygon to make a word.
■ Now write two new words from each polygon. Use the highlighted letter in each word.

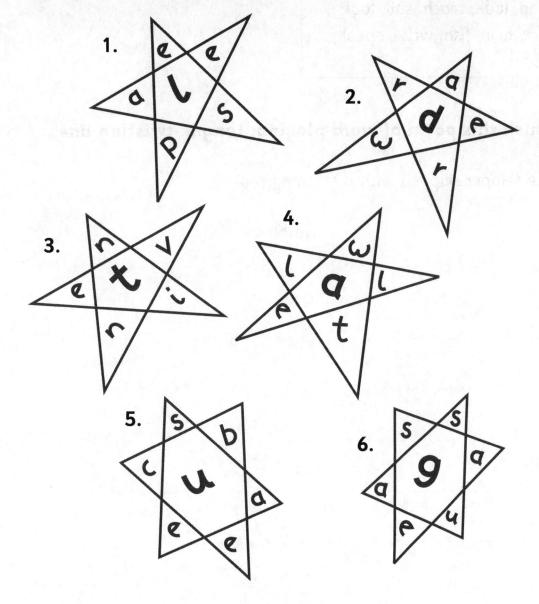

1. ....

2. ....

3. ....

4. ....

5. ....

6. ....

■SCHOLASTIC
www.scholastic.co.uk
59

PHOTOCOPIABLES

PHOTOCOPIABLE

Name _____   Date _____

Same start, different finish

Helpful words

farm, skip, play, work, shop, hop, look, teach, sail, look, act, help, fish, write, speak, care

Helpful word endings

er, s, es, ing, ed, ly, ful

Finish this poem of word-playing, tongue-twisting lines.

The skipper skipped with a skipping rope.

.... working, ...

....

....

....

....

....

....

....

....

DAILY SPELLING TEASERS FOR AGES 7–11

Name _____   Date _____

Negative thinking

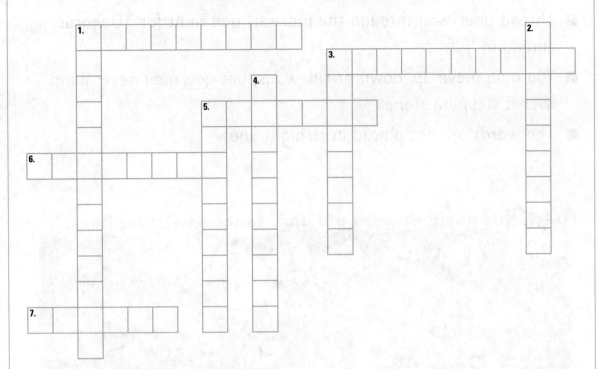

Across

1. This answer is not right

3. Cannot be done

5. Not within the law

6. Not the proper way to behave

7. Not like something

Down

1. Has no sense of responsibility

2. It cannot be read

3. Is not very active

4. Cannot read or write

5. At no fixed times

Name _____ Date _____

Maze rescue!

◖ Thread your way through the maze as you hunt for 10 words ending in 'ful'.

◖ You may move up, down or sideways, but you may never jump over a stepping stone.

◖ The words are not placed in straight lines.

DAILY SPELLING TEASERS FOR AGES 7–11

Name _____ Date _____

It's a match!

do not	I am	will not
there has	I have	cannot
you would	you have	he will
she would	does not	it will
I'm	you've	she'd
it'll	don't	you'd
he'll	there's	doesn't
won't	I've	can't

■SCHOLASTIC
www.scholastic.co.uk

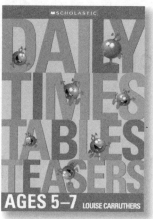

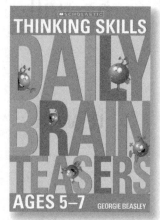